THINK BEYOND ARCHITECTURE: EVIDENCE BASED DESIGN APPROACH TO EXPLORE THE INDIAN VERNACULAR ARCHITECTURE

"THE THINK BEYOND ARCHITECTURE SERIES"

SAPTARSHI SANKAR CHAKRABARTI

Copyright © Saptarshi Sankar Chakrabarti
All Rights Reserved.

To the 'Architects' of the Future.

SAPTARSHI SANKAR CHAKRABARTI

Contents

What's Within The Covers?

Absolutely unputdownable and essential!

Crafted for the students of Architecture, Researchers of the subject, Human Settlement planners and Vernacular Architecture enthusiasts, this particular Book of the THINK BEYOND ARCHITECTURE Series, titled "Evidence Based Design Approach to Explore the Indian Vernacular Architecture.", Authored by Professor Architect SAPTARSHI SANKAR CHAKRABARTI, is the first of its kind in this segment, seeking uncommon answers to common questions, inspired by some simple principles of Aristotle's timeless and fundamental questioning framework, which is considered as the very basic foundations for information gathering in a Scientific Knowledge seeking scenario.

Book Objectives:

1. The Book looks at some specific Vernacular Architectural Communities of India.
2. The Book identifies and interprets specific local, regional, and national Vernacular traditions from India.
3. The Book develops a broader sense of understanding of the relationship between Architecture, Environment, and culture.
4. The Book emphasizes the importance and draws a parallel between Vernacular Architecture and the Sustainable Development Goals.

Built around the concept of thinking beyond the realm of Mainstream Architecture and Traditional Architectural Education, this Book is infused with personal introspections of the Author who takes us to a Deep Dive into the reality of the World we inhabit, and our spatial relation to the Vernacular Architecture of our civilization, through an Evidence Based Design ideation perspective. Approaching to decipher the multifaceted styles of Indian Vernacular Architecture, this Book dares to exhibit a uniquely engaging and emotionally involved Technical narrative, by Design.

The Author goes on to explore some of the highly intriguing Styles of Indian Vernacular Architecture, which is designed based on local needs, availability of construction materials, reflecting local traditions and climate. The Author shares his insight into the fundamental thinking beyond Architecture, relevant in the given case for our civilization, about an evidence based approach which evolved not through the practice of formally schooled Architects, but by the evidence based creative learning skills and traditions of local people.

Sharing his own multinational expertise of putting together the context, the methods, the practices, the principles, the tools and the techniques, in this particular book of the series, the Author explores an eye opening perspective towards the Evidence Based Design approach to understanding the styles of Indian Vernacular Architecture, which not only becomes absolutely useful while designing the future built environment in a more sustainable way, but also from the industry's perspective of practicality and real life hands-on implementability at the ground level.

Happy reading!

Reviews & Accolades

Great things never come from comfort zones.

Every human being is entitled to courtesy and consideration. If you're not open to constructive criticism, then you're not open to truly growing as a person. Therefore, honest Reviews and constructive criticism should not only to be expected, but should be actively sought, because you tend to learn more from your Failures than from your Successes.

"Wise people prefer to benefit from constructive criticism rather than be ruined by false praise. - Shiv Khera"

Reviews and comments are important. Constructive criticism evokes a sense of desire in us to perform, which then becomes the starting point of all achievement, not a hope, not a wish, but a keen pulsating desire, which transcends everything, because the game we love and enjoy, we can never lose.

BOOK-1 (THINK BEYOND ARCHITECTURE: ACHIEVING SUSTAINABILITY BY INTELLIGENT DESIGN, FOR A FUTURE PROOF SMART CITY)

BOOK-2 (THINK BEYOND ARCHITECTURE: HOW TO FIGHT THE FUTURE AND FIND YOUR OWN SHORTCUT TO SUCCESS IN DESIGN STUDIOS, THESIS PROJECTS AND CAREER)

All that we enjoy and love deeply becomes a part of us. Resilience and continuity therefore becomes the key to success. Without a resilient and continual growth along with progress, such words as improvement, achievement, and success have no meaning. Also it is equally important to be thankful for the valuable feedback and blessings which is received. Being thankful and expressing your gratitude is an important part of being happy in life, because when we start counting our blessings, our whole life turns around. Winston Churchill had once said, that we make a living by what we get, but we make a life by what we give. Enclosed herein are some kind words of inspiration and constructive comments on this particular Series of Books, as were shared by many renowned stalwarts of the industry and academia:

Executive Reviews: Referenced from previous publications of the THINK BEYOND ARCHITECTURE Series of books.

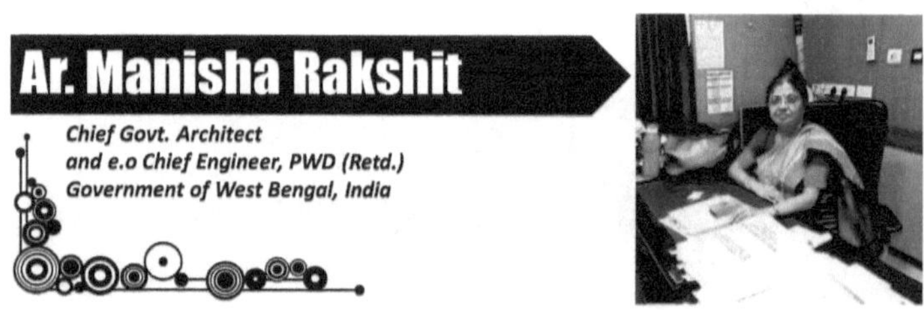

Review Note: 001

I have gone through the book, "Think beyond Architecture", achieving Sustainability by Intelligent Design, for a Future Proof Smart City, written by Prof. Dr. SAPTARSHI SANKAR CHAKRABARTI. I know that he has a vast experience on many practical projects, as well as he is a good teacher.

The subject matter described in this book has followed the guidelines of the National Smart Cities Mission, an Urban Renewal Program by the Government of India.

The appreciated parts of the writings are that, they have focused on the Mission to develop the Economic Growth and improve the quality of lifestyle of the people by developing Local Areas and make use of Natural Resources especially to preserve Energy that leads to a Smart City. It was also described about the evils of the Urbanization with Human Settlement.

The problems and solutions of Urban Areas have been described in detail, especially regarding Unemployment, Transport, Water, Sewage, Garbage, Health and Pollution.

The Sustainability in the Urban Areas, have been described through the eyes of an Architect. The Sustainable Urbanization, starting with Green Building concept and the Livelihood Pattern, have been explained in a very logical manner.

He has also considered the essential changes in order to achieve the Sustainability for creating a Future Proof Smart City, in New Normal Life after Covid-19 Pandemic. I think the author should write another book, only on this issue.

This book is very much helpful and a very good reference to the Students of Architecture, Urban Designers, City Planners, etc.

Last, but not the least, I must say, the Cover Design, which is also designed by the author himself, is excellent. The design composition and the color of the cover page made me spell bound.

I think the expectation of the readers will grow from more to more.

I wish the young author success in life.

- Ar. Manisha Rakshit

****

Prof.Dr.Manik Gopal Som

Former Vice-Chancellor, BCKV, West Bengal, India.
Recipient of National Silver Jubilee plaque,
Fellow & Life member of Indian Society of Veg. Science,
Life member of Adv. of Horti. Society, India

Review Note: 002

Now a days, ecological engineering is a concept based on which the Smart Cities/ towns are being planned where the nature and human society stay in harmony. Architecture is an important central theme within an ecological context, with reference to planning the Architecture and its built environment. Holistic ecologic Architecture can lead us into a harmony of the desired nature and our society. In fact, Architecture and built environment are reflections of our society. Recently, I have gone through an interesting book entitled, "Think Beyond Architecture", written by Dr. Saptarshi Sankar Chakrabarti, which aims at promoting mass awareness regarding people's mainstream framework of understanding the ideas related to what these new age architectural interventions should really aim at, in terms of achieving sustainability by intelligent design in making future smart cities.

I appreciate that Dr. Chakrabarti, an award winning Architect consultant, has taken great care to put together this incredible book which becomes the very first one of the series uniquely crafted for not only the students and academicians, but perhaps for one and all.

In this ten chapter book, Dr. Chakrabarti starts by mentioning about the 'One Dozen Evils' of our current urban livelihood, thereafter he goes on to analyzing 'The Indian Smart City Mission', which had become the talk of the town at our recent times. Further, he addresses the issues related to Sustainable Architecture for which the world has started critically looking back to the twentieth century activities relating to the subject. The immediate past has not contributed much in this respect. He has also emphasized about the design of Urban Architecture based on ecologic ethics i.e., creating Architecture with nature.

Dr. Chakrabarti also shares his experiences in experimenting with future urban agriculture practicing the concept of responsible intelligent ideas like 'AGRITECTURE', a well balanced mixture of AGRICULTURE and ARCHITECTURE.

He urges upon the future generation of Architects to Think Beyond Architecture and get ready to the new world with eco-friendly designs which Dr. Chakrabarti has outlined in this book. He has also exhibited sincere dedication and hard work in authoring this book with this new idea of 'Agritecture' or in other words which we can call as holistic ecologic Architecture.

I am sure that this book will be an important source of information on Architecture and ecological engineering for tropical countries.

- Prof. Dr. Manik Gopal Som

****

Mr. Anup S. Bhattacharya

Former Chairman and Managing Director, Bank of Maharashtra and Former Chairman, Institute of Banking Personnel Selection, Maharashtra, India

Review Note: 003

It is very interesting to read the Book titled, "Think Beyond Architecture", authored by Prof. Dr. Saptarshi Sankar Chakrabarti, an eminent Architect with experience of more than a decade. The Book has Ten Chapters from Evils in the society to New Normal Blueprint for the Society. The objective of the Book is to highlight the society evils to resolutions.

Public, Politicians, Administrators must read this Book for the benefit of Community in particular.

The proverb says "ROTI, KAPRA and MOKAN" are three basic necessities for human life. In Developing Countries ROTI (Food) and KAPRA (Clothes) are mostly now available. But MOKAN (Shelter) with all amenities like Drinking water, Sanitary toilets, Pucca Roads, Adequate Electricity etc are rarely available. India is not the exception. 'One Dozen Evils' as rightly explained in lucid and simple sentences, correctly point out the contradictions amongst the community, Rulers, implementers. Now we cannot think "Son of Farmers will engage in farming in the villages only where proper infrastructure seems to be lacking". In this era of Internet/ mobile/TV everyone is aware of what has been happening in other parts of the world. Everyone likes to step into urban areas for Infrastructure comfort, Education, Employment opportunity etc. As a result, urban areas are over crowed and existing inhabitants are devoid of proper amenities /infrastructure. SPORADIC FLATS, HOUSES are being constructed to accommodate influx of people without taking care of One Dozen Devils, as narrated in the first chapter of the Book.

Thanks to Prof. Dr. Saptarshi Sankar Chakrabarti for authoring such a "Points to Ponder" Book.

In true sense, it is not possible to take care of proper infrastructure under such influx from village to Urban areas including Migratory Labors for Employment. If we are allowed to analyze three Cities now – Bengaluru, Kolkata and Mumbai. Other cities may be analyzed also. Since I am more familiar with these three cities, I like to compare such cities in the 70s and now. Bengaluru was called SWITZERLAND with calm, quite, humming sound etc. Now it is mostly crowded with Traffic jam, Pollution, Sewerage issues and sporadic construction of High Rise Buildings etc. Bengaluru Administration is not in a position to manage infrastructure. Kolkata and Mumbai are also facing the same issues and problems.

IF WE DO NOT TAKE CORRECTIVE STEPS NOW, THERE WILL BE FIGHT, BLOOD SHEDS IN VIEW OF OVER CROWDING.

IT has been depicted and suggested very well by Dr. Chakrabarti. Sporadic constructions of HIGH RISE BUILDINGS are to be avoided. Concept of SMART GREEN CITY in the Semi Urban, Urban, Rural areas should be thought of in phases with proper Infrastructure facilities. In Urban, Semi urban areas where Farming in true sense is not possible but scope of kitchen gardens, BEE keeping, Pot vegetable cultivation of daily needs in roof tops, back yard etc. are possible.

This has been given a very suitable nomenclature "AGRITECTURE = AGRICULTURE + ARCHITECTURE".

Thinking is very simple but difficult to implement. This may be implemented provided (i) Architects (ii) Politicians (iii) Rule Makers and Implementers and (iv) Community people seriously deliberate on these issues, focused elaborately in the Book and DEVILS may be changed to BLESSINGS in a decade or two.

- Mr. Anup Sankar Bhattacharya

****

Review Note: 004

Recently I had the pleasure of going through a publication titled Think Beyond Architecture authored by Dr. Saptarshi Sankar Chakrabarti, Professor and researcher and a professional of global repute, in the field of Architecture. Having read the book with interest, I have found it reflective of the author's sound knowledge and intense scholarship besides his analytical skill and incisive thinking.

The book seems to be based on extensive research carried out in regard to the Art and Science of Architecture.

The book begins with a chapter which is titled quite interestingly as One Dozen Evils. This chapter refers to a number of issues like Overcrowding, Unemployment, Slums & Squatter Settlements, Water Supply, Sewerage, Trash Disposal, Human Health and Pollution etc., which have perennially challenged the discipline of Architecture. These issues do not only circumscribe Architecture as a human endeavor, but also provide a perspective to any meaningful discourse on the subject. It is therefore in the fitness of things that the author has chosen to place these issues at the beginning of his fascinating book.

I was impressed by the scope and coverage of the book.

It covers almost everything that Architecture may even remotely pertain to. Some of the chapters like Sustainability in the Urban Precinct, Creating Architecture with Nature, Future-Proof Urban Agriculture and Responsible Intelligent Design etc., indeed have universal appeal. The chapter titled The Indian Smart City Mission, contains points which according to the present reviewer can be of great operational significance to the professionals currently engaged in carrying forward the Smart City Mission across India. The world is becoming increasingly conscious of the imperatives of Sustainability. It is, therefore, quite appropriate that the book under review has examined different aspects of Sustainability in considerable depth. For instance, it refers to the Three Pillars of Sustainability, namely, Social Equity, Economic Viability and Environmental Protection and analyses how Architecture can be oriented to the need of striking a balance across these three pillars (vide Chapter 3 titled Sustainability in the Urban Precinct).

The approach adopted in the book on this subject is visibly in tune with the Sustainable Development Goals announced by the United Nations in 2015, which are knitted in an integrated and indivisible frame aimed at securing a balance among the above-mentioned Three Dimensions of Sustainable Development. Another remarkable feature of this book is its sensitivity to the issues that concern millions of under-privileged, while not losing sight of debates centred around Architecture as one of the most significant pillars of a country's growth and development. The chapter titled Affordable Housing for a Smart City is an example in hand.

The extraordinary situation which has emerged in the entire world in the wake of the COVID-19 pandemic- often described as the state of The New Normal, has not escaped the attention of the perceptive author.

As such, an entire chapter with the title The New Normal Blueprint is devoted to discuss ways and means for addressing the challenges thrown up by this unprecedented development.

Author in this chapter quite appropriately states "Agility, Flexibility and Adaptability shall be the New Normal Mantra."

This book is refreshingly different from the usual literature on similar subjects, for it is far from being esoteric. The book does not appear to be narrow or sectarian in approach, hence the title of the book: Think Beyond Architecture. The book is by no means inscrutable. Rather it is amazingly readable. No wonder, I could go through the book with engaging attention and sustained interest, and obtain valuable insights from it, although I am not professionally trained in this discipline. I believe anyone interested in the Art and Science of design and construction of buildings and allied matters, even though not having formal training in the subject, can venture to go through this interesting book with the hope of coming back with a great deal of take-aways.

That is so because the book is deep in analysis and lucid in exposition, besides being comprehensive in coverage and contemporary in focus.

- Prof. Prabal Kumar Sen

****

Review Note: 005

Written by Professor Dr. Saptarshi Sankar Chakrabarti, the book "THINK BEYOND ARCHITECTURE" arrives at an opportune moment. The growing worldwide realization of the need for Sustainable Development, gives this volume abundant timeliness and relevancy.

The book is a resource for Government and Industry as well as a text for the students of Architecture.

The book contains worked-out example problems illustrating Architectural analysis from a system perspective and problem sets to reinforce concepts and applications.

The author covers Indian Smart City Mission in depth, as it is considered one of the most important requirements for building a Sustainable Future.

- Prof. Dr. S. P. Gon Chaudhuri

****

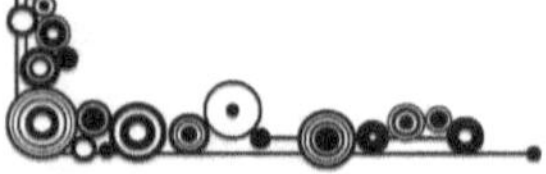

Review Note: 006

I have been highly impressed by the book "Think Beyond Architecture" by Dr. Saptarshi Sankar Chakrabarti.

He has a lucid way of handling highly technical issues related to Sustainability, Future Proofing of Smart Cities etc.

The beauty is, he is around all along, in interaction leaving a personal touch as he explains different aspects of development. A mention is made of 'cordless elevators' of the future, in high-rise buildings using maglev technique.

An important point is raised by the author; by the time the team of Architects reaches a project site, lush green forests have already been burnt down.

The damage is done by following the rules rather than by breaking them. It is a dilemma for practicing executives indeed.

It has been a pleasant and rewarding reading.

I eagerly look forward to the next release in the series.

- Mr. Dibakar Chakrabarti

****

Dr. Gopendu B.Chowdhury

M.V.Sc. (Agra), Ex-Joint Director,
Animal Resources Development Dept.,
Government of Tripura, India

Review Note: 007

Recently I have received one book named, "Think Beyond Architecture", a Series authored by Dr. Saptarshi Sankar Chakrabarti, globally released through the prestigious Amazon International Platform publication on the 15th of August 2020.

Professor Chakrabarti, in the very first page said about the purpose of writing this book. The purpose was "for achieving sustainability by intelligent design, for a future proof smart city". He further said that there will be a series of books themed as the "Think Beyond Architecture" Series. In this book he dealt with Architecture first and then with Urban Agriculture.

He has proposed a totally new and unique subject: Agritecture (Architecture + Agriculture) and hoped that the subject will be taught in colleges and universities in future.

He believes that it does not need to be a star Architect for a classical Architectural design. He wishes to see people having pragmatic wisdom for Urban Designing of a Smart City. Professor, being author, while writing the book he might have thought of his students. In fact, the book appears to be written for the students. His English wordings are very simple and lucid. His way of writing is very straight forward.

He emphatically says "I practice what I preach"!

Smart cities are coming up in India and also in other countries. Urban Architecture will be in great demand if there is proper implementation of Smart City schemes.

I am sure, this book, for novelty of its approach, will be liked by many.

I cannot restrain myself without telling something about the childhood of Professor Chakrabarti. In his childhood, he used to come to our house occasionally. I used to tell him different stories every day. After hearing those stories, he used to ask me a lot of intelligent questions. He used to play with various unique items and they weren't very common. We all know the proverb that 'Morning shows the Day'. This was appropriate for him in his early childhood. Seeing him like this, we easily acknowledged and realized that his future was very bright. He is yet to reach to his zenith. My love and blessings will remain for him always.

- Dr. Gopendu Bhusan Chowdhury

****

Review Note: 008

It gives immense pleasure to read such an informative book after a long time. In fact it is a handbook for an Urban

Designer. Very well described about various elements of Smart City design and Sustainable Development Goals.

As a Professional Architect, sometimes we are busy satisfying client's demand, but this book reminds me to Think Beyond Architecture and Creating Architecture with Nature.

I congratulate Architect Dr. Saptarshi Sankar Chakrabarti for penning down such a fabulous book!

- Ar. Taskir Hussain

****

Review Note: 009

The book titled, "Think Beyond Architecture" will attract considerable attention of students, researchers, consultants and others who are dealing with Architecture and other allied subjects. The writer discussed many allied things related to architectural planning in the present perspective, taking into consideration urban planning in general and city and country planning as a whole, that is why the title of the book "Think Beyond Architecture" is appropriate.

The Chapters (1 to 10) included in the Book, contains information which are thought provoking and very useful.

The author pointed out the importance of food production in the form of vegetables, floriculture, arboriculture and animal husbandry using local resources and their distribution and marketing under one umbrella. The idea of roof top garden, gardening through hydroponics and mention of vertical farming are very interesting.

The book contains over three hundred effective pages with more than a hundred technical abbreviations, around hundred technical references and a brief epilogue indicating future directions.

I appreciate the hard work done by the author and his vision about the future Sustainable Smart Cities.

I wish to see a wide circulation of this highly useful and interesting Book.

- Mr. Sibir Kumar Laha

****

**Former Chief Marine Engineer,
Urban Organic Farming Practitioner and
Mentor, Alternative Livelihood & Agriculture, India**

Review Note: 010

God has created human beings, with super intellectual abilities as his best creation. Therefore, it is human beings who can lift themselves above nature with their super consciousness and become God. At the same time, they can go down by inviting the destructive devices to destroy for meeting the demand of their unlimited greed and for gaining personal needs. This unlimited greed is leading the universe towards destruction of the natural fabrics. Huge number of cities, unplanned and without need to maintain the natural balance, are coming up which will lead to disaster. Planning must be done in harmony with the experiences of the practical field researchers, visualizing real-time conditions and implemented without being pressurized or motivated for small gains. Recently, I have come across a book, "Think Beyond Architecture" authored by Dr. Saptarshi Sankar Chakrabarti, who is an Architect by profession and also a Professor in the University. Based on his practical experience of about two decades, he has in an wonderful manner, pointed out the evils of unplanned urbanization and the ways to overcome the shortcomings by assimilating the noble ideas of Architecture, Agriculture, and other related subjects for building up new age cities compatible with nature.

He has nicely coined a term, "Agritecture" by synthesizing Agriculture with Architecture for motivating the people in general, to Think Beyond Architecture and go for a Green Sustainable Development.

The book has been written in a lucid language, avoiding mainstream technical terms and giving a joyful feeling while reading.

I believe, this book will attract the fancy of many readers and provide thought, not only to Architects but also to Planners, Administrators and others for a new horizon of thinking.

My hearty appreciation is due to the author for his hard work in assimilating various ideas and thoughts by going through a huge number of references and his practical experiences. I have high opinion that the book will be liked by many people across the globe and will push forward towards a Sustainable, Healthy and Environment Friendly Living. I wish to see many such books from the author, which will provide fuel for new thoughts.

   - Mr. Subhas Ch. Mondal

****

M.Sc (Agri), BCKV (Bidhan Chandra Krishi Viswavidyalaya / Bidhan Chandra Agricultural University) West Bengal, India

Review Note: 011

I recently had the opportunity to go through a highly interesting book, 'Think Beyond Architecture', authored by Dr. Saptarshi Sankar Chakrabarti and Internationally launched on the 15th of August 2020, with the ISBN Mark.

It is amazing to note that a man of Architecture envisages to 'Think Beyond Architecture'!

This prompted me to go through the book with sheer interest. At the outset, various problems faced by the present day cities / towns all over the world in general and India in particular has been elucidated vividly. To tackle the virulent problems of unplanned urbanization and, inter alia, emphasizing on conservation of environment, utilizing I.T support and human (citizens) participation, a smart solution has been adopted by GOI to establish / encourage the formation of Smart Cities. Smart Cities Mission aspires to develop living spaces characterized by ease of Living, Education, Employment, Economy and Entertainment with an ultimate object to improve quality of life. Here arises the matter Sof Sustainability of the situation perpetually in future and is capable to meet present day needs as well as needs of the future generations.

The author has very nicely elaborated the pros and cons of Sustainability, which mainly depends on maintenance of equilibrium among its three legs viz., Economic, Social and Environmental.

The greatest challenge, I think, lies in regard to conservation of natural resources / environment vis-à-vis entire development process. Political good will plays a major role in this regard. While building Smart Cities, the question of affordability arises along with sustainability. There is huge demand for affordable housing mainly amongst the economically weaker sections of the society. Author has duly indicated the ways and methods / principles to be followed for constructing green affordable energy efficient buildings with the optimum utilization of local resources including active human participation. He has further emphasized that human psychology is directly related to Architecture. Built environment affects human beings mentally and physically. So he advocated that future smart cities should be designed suitably for the ease of the people living there using all relevant data / evidence available without hurting the nature / environment rather, combating the climate change. Here the author dives deep into the nature and urges to listen to the unique sounds of Sustainable nature and its uncontrollable beauty of harmony and to incorporate the lessons from nature in the Architectural design, so that humans living in the built environment can feel and smell the nature to its maximum for their physiological and psychological betterment. He feels helpless intense pains observing the huge destruction of nature for building cities / Architectural constructions. So he urges meaningfully to "Think Beyond Architecture", and in this juncture it is amazing to hear a new terminology

"Agritecture", combining Agriculture and Architecture.

Very interestingly the author intends to mould Architecture suitably to incorporate / facilitate the practice of Urban Agriculture which will not only support the Urban Food Security by making available quality organic fresh fruits and vegetables / animal products grown within smart city at cheaper price, but also help substantially reducing Carbon Foot Print due to lesser burning of fossil fuel for transporting the food articles from far off places to cities. This has immense effect on urban employment opportunity and economy and also helps fulfil various State and Central Govt. schemes creating green and clean city. This really fills us with joy and excitement that with this endeavor of Agritecture we are going to witness an urban green revolution soon, keeping in mind, the food safety of more than 50% of world populace living in cities and to offset the effect of climate change. Thus the author travels through various technological developments/ ideas / themes, not directly related to Architecture but needs urgent attention of the present day Architects for meaningful and vibrant Architectural designs to make Architecture for everyone. This is very much essential under this New Normal situation which demands a paradigm shift in traditional Architectural thoughts and ideas and now it is clearly understood the rational why an Architect urges to "Think beyond Architecture".

I think all will agree with this. Enjoyed the pleasant reading very much.

In the light of the above discussion, I express my sincere thanks and gratitude to the author for presenting us this book, written in a very palatable and interesting manner, at his maiden endeavor and expect next issue of the series shortly.

I think this book is essential for reading by the people in general and Architectural Designers, Planners and Students in particular. At the same time, the book is very helpful for Agricultural Students and Research Fellows to have some insights on further / ongoing technological improvement in the field of urban farming to suit the Architectural designs / planning to maximize Urban Organic production.

This book, I think, will also be adorned by the Environmentalists for obvious reasons.

I appreciate the author, who had been an academician and a practicing Architect for the last two decades, for this huge painstaking endeavor of assimilating the noble ideas of Architecture, Agriculture and allied subjects. I wish the author further success in life.

- Mr. Swapan Kr. Bhowmik

****

Review Note: 012

While reading a book, the reader might contemplate, at the age of internet, when most of the information on any topic is available in the net, what is the reason/ purpose for writing a book on Architecture covering Environment, Urban Agriculture etc. I think the target group is the Students of Architecture.

The author with his vast knowledge and wide experience has compiled most of the information related to the topic under the cover of "Think Beyond Architecture", so that the students and other interested persons will easily understand.

They need not to search internet for requisite information. The author has touched all most all the issues related to the subject.... The author has succeeded in bringing all the related issues for sustainable development of future cities.

After reading the book, the reader will have clear mind and even if he is not directly connected with the planning of a future city, as a concerned citizen of the country, may raise his voice pointing out the lacuna of a project.

- Dr. Subrata Bhowmik

****

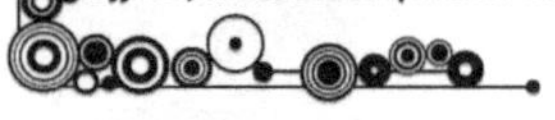

Review Note: 013

As a result of unplanned urbanization, there has been substantial damage of ecology and caused unsustainable growth. There is gradual deterioration and degradation of ecology, which has been a cause of concern to the Scientists and Environmentalists.

Time is ripe to think differently to save our mother earth and the human civilization from ecological disaster.

Therefore, it is urgently necessary to shift our focus of planning from the stereotype mainstream planning, particularly, the urban Planning with a long-term view.

Very recently, I have gone through a Book, "Think Beyond Architecture", written by Dr. Saptarshi Sankar Chakrabarti, a Professor and a practicing Architect for the last two decades. The Book was published globally on 15th August 2020, with ISBN mark, which deals in detail, in its ten separate chapters, the evils of present urbanization and the root causes of the same and the alternative avenues to combat the degradation.

He has very nicely explained it in a lucid and simple language with a view to promote awareness in the people's understanding of the ideas and innovative concept of new age Architectural intervention that should aim at sustainability by intelligent design for making futuristic planning and design of urban cities.

Dr. Chakrabarti dealt with a dozens of evils in our present urban livelihood scenario and elaborated the 'Smart City mission', which has become the talk of the town in the present day context. He has also highlighted the issues related to the Sustainability in the Urban Prescient, Affordable housing for the Smart Cities, 'Evidence Based Design in urban Architecture' and creating Architecture more relevant to nature and nature friendly along with other issues.

The Author has shared his decades of hand on experience after experimenting with 'Future Proof Urban Agriculture', practicing and preaching the concept of 'Responsible Intelligent Design'.

Being an Agricultural professional, I have worked in different capacities and different institutions of India and the Royal Government of Bhutan, in the Rural and Urban

Environment. I have also spent more than 21 years in Sundarbans in the Capacity of the Chief Executive Officer, Resources Development Foundation (a Non-Government Organization).

I have been fascinated by the unique idea coined in the word "AGRITECTURE", which is a balanced mix of Agriculture and Architecture.

As per assertion of Pluto: "Books give soul to the universe, wings to the mind, flight to the imagination and life for everything." The book most probably covered all these issues.

I appreciate the hard work and care the Author has taken to put together the ideas and concepts in this incredible book, which is the first one in the series.

I understand the book has attracted attention of many people across the country and has already created a demand.

I extend my best wishes to the author for his effort to make it lucid and attractive and with a beautiful cover, designed by himself.

This would be a good book for reference to the Students, Teachers and the Researchers.

I wish Dr. Chakrabarti all the Success.

- Dr. Tushar Kanti Ghosh

****

Former Senior Executive, State Bank of India
M.Sc(Agri), Ph.D (Bidhan Chandra Krishi
Viswavidyalaya / Bidhan Chandra Agricultural
University, West Bengal, India).

Review Note: 014

In a developing country, like India, urbanisation at a faster rate is inevitable. Urbanisation is a sign of progress and development of a country. But, urbanisation without proper and systematic planning, as had been done in old cities of India, lead to a number of socio-economic and environmental problems.

The book, "Think Beyond Architecture", in its ten chapters, elaborately dealt all these problems and identified how these problems affect the livelihood of the urban population.

Another serious concern, because of unplanned urban growth is rapid depletion of precious agricultural land. The author in this book, based on his two decades of experience as Professor in a university and his practicing experience in this line, emphasised on sound city planning and development of "Smart City", to overcome all these problems as faced by the cities of India at present.

The book is a vision document for future cities of India.

It has brought some concepts, which are beyond the thinking of common people. Concept of Smart City, which means sustainable development of Smart Cities of future, balancing the basic needs of sustainability on social, environmental and economic fronts. The book also narrates concept of "Smart Housing", which means providing housing for poor and middle-income group in the cities, at affordable prices. For this purpose, the author focuses on the idea of "Think Globally, Act Locally" i.e. to source all the materials and technology locally for constructing houses at affordable prices.

The author also coined a unique idea of "AGRITECTURE", combining the related points of

"AGRICULTURE" and "ARCHITECTURE". It defines home as both shelters and food. The book discussed the idea in depth.

In fine, I like to mention that the book, 'ThinkBeyond Architecture', is a well-researched book providing a lot of relevant information and data to the readers relating to the good ideas of Smart Cities with Sustainable Development of urban India.

This is a unique book of its kind and an eye opener for the future developed Indian Cities.

I appreciate the hard labour the author has undertaken for writing the book after consulting a number of research papers and related books and also assimilating his own experience of teaching and practicing the subject for two decades.

If I am to give scoring of the book, I shall rate 5 out of 5 marks to the author for this noble work.

I wish wide circulation of the book and success of the author.

- Dr. Naba Kumar Kolay

****

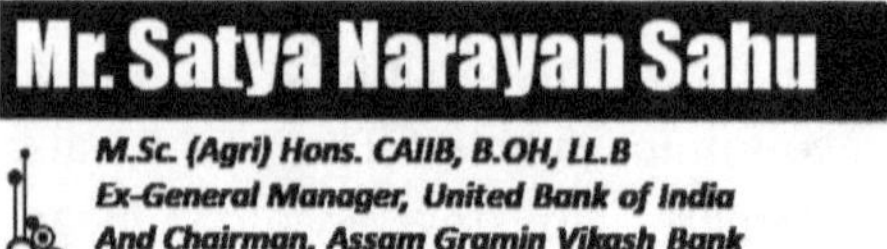

Review Note: 015

Recently, I got a chance to read a book, "Think Beyond Architecture", written by Dr. Saptarshi Sankar Chakrabarti.

Since I had been a student of Agricultural Engineering in early days and acquired sound knowledge of Architecture during my service carrier, in different capacities in Banking Sector due to Professional Demand.

When I started reading the book, its topics and their details compelled me to continue to read the whole book due to its amazing contents, explanations, suggestions and experience of the author in writing the book.

In my opinion 'Think Beyond Architecture' is a marvellous book authored by Dr. Chakrabarti covering specific and proper aspects of Architecture meant for town and city planning.

This book is like a handbook on the subject and must be read by Students as well as Professional Architects.

I wish all the best to Prof. Dr. Saptarshi Sankar Chakrabarti for his Careers and also request him to continue writing on the subject for enabling the readers to get the opportunity of having similar informative and enjoyable reading experience.

- Mr. Satya Narayan Sahu

****

Introduction

SAPTARSHI SANKAR CHAKRABARTI

ARCHITECT, AUTHOR, ADVISOR; Keynote Speaker (International), Professor Dr. SAPTARSHI SANKAR CHAKRABARTI, is an Independent Chartered Consulting Architect by Profession, a Smart City Specialist (Intelligent Urban Solutions & Sustainable Architecture), an Indian Green Building Council Accredited Professional (IGBC™-AP), seasoned over two decades of hands-on experience in spearheading numerous Multidisciplinary Projects, undertaking Research and Development, and actively Mentoring throughout the domain of Architecture, Interior Design, Urban Design, Master Planning, Landscaping, Green Buildings and Smart City Mission projects across India and abroad.

Apart from being an eminent Industry Consultant, a Serial Entrepreneur, a Thought Leader and a Mentor, operating extensively throughout South Asia and beyond, Professor Dr. SAPTARSHI SANKAR CHAKRABARTI had also been recognized for continually Mentoring the industry as a Sector/Trade Expert, by the Ministry of Skill Development and Entrepreneurship (MSDE), Government of India.

Recognized for promoting Industry-Academia interfacing and sustainable practices in the region, Professor Dr. SAPTARSHI SANKAR CHAKRABARTI, had been a creative and passionate designer by training; with outstanding conceptualization skills that are driven by Evidence Based Design (EBD) methodology, Intelligent Bioclimatic Design (IBD) approach, implementable Research & Development; having a substantial track record of 100% Completed projects from concept to commissioning, throughout his highly colorful career.

Focused on a benevolent Global Mission of making the World a better place by continually creating Innovative Sustainable Design Solutions and Mentoring future Architects, he had been Public Speaking and Authoring regularly across various online and offline platforms, in order to widely share his expertise with the World; while his rich creative achievement background, in academics as well as in profession, being continually endowed with several regional and national awards, on the go.

Registered with the Indian Council of Architecture (COA), Professor Dr. SAPTARSHI SANKAR CHAKRABARTI had always been sought after for being a highly resourceful technical professional, having excellent interpersonal communication skills with proven abilities in networking and establishing long term client relationships with public and private institutions.

He had been actively associated with significant professional bodies of the industry, like the Indian Council of Architecture (COA), the Institute of Indian Interior Designers (IIID), the Institute of Urban Designers India (IUDI), the Indian Green Building Council (IGBC), the Indian Institute of Architects (IIA), Zoo Authority of India (CZA, Government of India), Ministry of Tourism (Government of India), Ministry of Skill Development and Entrepreneurship (MSDE, Government of India), Development Authorities, Smart City Corporations, other Public Departments of the Government of West Bengal and many more.

He can be quickly reached through any of the following links given here.

Mobile/ WhatsApp:
+91 9477586654
Email ID/ Google-Profile:
sschakrabarti@gmail.com
Social Media/ Global Network:
https://www.linkedin.com/in/saptarshischakrabarti/
https://www.facebook.com/sschakrabarti.fanpage/
https://www.youtube.com/saptarshichakrabarti/
https://www.instagram.com/architectsaptarshi/
https://www.twitter.com/ss_chakrabarti/

Preface

Vernacular Architecture originated when mankind started to provide itself shelter according to its circumstances, made from surrounding materials. It is a mere response to society's needs that has allowed man to construct climate-responsive structures even before the Architects.

Such simple traditions have long been regarded as backward and seemingly forgotten in modern Architecture, but are catching eyes back, as these structures have proven to be energy-efficient and altogether sustainable. During this time of rapid technological advancement and urbanization, there is still much to be learned from the traditional knowledge of vernacular construction.

What is Vernacular Architecture?

According to its etymology, "Verna" means native and "Architecture" is to design buildings, thus vernacular architecture is an architecture style that is built to meet the present needs, keeping in mind the local climate, culture, and materials. But its presence appeared a long time back when the need for "a shelter" had risen, which pushed humans to use indigenous techniques and materials to formulate an optimum solution for themselves. This gave birth to a "tent" that now has innumerable design options.

Since then this field is evolving yet dispersed. It is evolving because the local conditions proportionally evolve and dispersed because it is purely regional, and its diverse nature makes it difficult to be propounded into a singular style with a name. It is in contradiction to the aesthetical and modern architecture of the present times.

Vernacular Architecture ©Nadejda Aliénor Illustration

In the 1800s, the term Vernacular was looked down upon and was used for an entity that was ordinary and designed out of necessity. In 1964 an exhibition was held by Bernard Rudofsky, called "Architecture without Architects", this very event established the significance of the term "vernacular architecture" amongst the architects, which was followed by amplification by ace architects like Le Corbusier, Adolf Loos, and Frank Lloyd Wright.

> "*As Frank Lloyd Wright says, we have to create an architecture that speaks for its time and place and yet yearns for timelessness.*"

An Architect cannot and should not create spaces without sensitivity and awareness towards the historical interventions, making it imperative to understand the factors that help designing spaces that are contextual with the surroundings and yet eternal.

With the onset of modern architecture, the latest technologies and construction methods and manufactured and processed materials became a norm, but in reality, they are energy drainers and impact the environment on huge levels. On the contrary, vernacular architecture is sustainable in its approach and uses green building techniques to work around its design schemes. It works on techniques that lower the carbon footprint, hence reducing the pressure on the environment.

For example, the Warli House in Maharashtra uses karvi stones to create a light external envelope that quickly dissipates the internal heat creating a cool interior atmosphere in a hot and humid climate of the central plain. Another example of a climate-responsive building style is the Bhonga House, which is a typical Rajasthani circular house that has thick mud walls, protecting the inmates from the hot and arid climate of the desert city. Taking a cue from the above studies Modo Designs have designed a house known as The House of Courtyards in Ahmedabad, which has been built on the concept of "pols", typical to the city's vernacular architecture, where a "pol" was a cluster of houses around a courtyard that has a common entrance and also gives protection from the harsh weather conditions by sufficing cross-ventilation. This house is built around a series of open courts that create a tunnel effect in the interiors and create a cool atmosphere.

Vernacular architecture was the informal style of building the houses for the needs of people using local materials. In vernacular Architecture there was a use of the local resources and land were used in the best way possible. In modern technology-based Architecture the resources are available everywhere but sometimes these resources are not eco-friendly for the particular region. The modern technology design is far better than the vernacular design but that modern technology is not enough to meet the needs of the local people. So, the Modern skillful architecture started to adapt the purpose of Vernacular Architecture. In ancient time the use of the local materials, local technologies in construction were a sustainable outcome according to the need. But with help of modern technology the ancient technology can achieve a more sustainable structure to mitigate the regional problem.

In my personal experience of working across South East Asia, I have observed that all cities nowadays have a repetitive Architectural monologue and have become a plethora of glass, concrete, and steel. They have parted ways with their local traditional Architecture, thus losing out on their originality. These cities are facing a major identity crisis. If vernacular architecture is allowed to play its role, the cultural landscape of a city can be protected, creating a dialogue between the city and its inhabitants.

Talking about India, it is a land full of assorted cultures that include festivals, religions, foods, attires, and occupations, thus breeding various examples of vernacular architecture. Some examples are the Havelis of Ahmedabad, the typical brick architecture of Chandigarh, or the houses in Himachal Pradesh, which have a separate room for grain storage, as agriculture is their major source of income and many others like them. Architects like Raj Rewal have also designed low-cost housings like the Aranya Housing in Madhya Pradesh on the lines of a typical Indian city that has narrow streets with congregational spaces to celebrate the culture of the city. Sadly, it's fading, the notion of modernity is overshadowing the need to protect the cultural heritage.

"While we are living in times when we can export and import materials nationally and internationally on a phone call, we also increase the cost of the project, which in turn creates a gap in the economic growth of the country."

In introspection, the Vernacular Architecture uses homegrown materials thus cutting down on various costs like the processing and manufacturing, the transport, and the cost of intricate construction processes for its application, then why not shift to a more local approach. These materials that are used depend on the location, they can be wooden in earthquake-prone regions and brick and clay in hot and humid climates.

Local people used the mud house as an appropriate solution for storage because it was cheap and available, and it could be insulated extremely well, which fit the needs of some residents. In 21st Century the idea of using adobe brick to construct was based on the ancient mud house so that it can be more sustainable and also the houses can be more eco-friendly in comparison to today's material.6000 years old material called cob is still an important material to build an organic farm. This cob is woven in crisscross pattern of wooden structure. From Vernacular to modern architecture the use of cob which is actually a composition of wet soil is very attractive. The advantage of the COB is that the architecture can give shape into their wish as the material is based on the wet soil. In old age of vernacular, the temperature of that region was also kept in mind during the making of the house. In Modern architecture some materials used in construction also depend on the topical region. As an example, an architect will use the white marble stone in construction at the hot and high humid location like desert area but not in cold breeze area or any hill station like Ooty. Thus, the use of white marble stone is an example of modern technology whereas choosing the appropriate location for the particular material is learnt from the vernacular architecture process. Stones are used widely instead of modern techniques of glass, concrete etc., as the different kinds of stones are more easily available in many regions than the above-mentioned modern materials. Benefits of using vernacular technology in modern architecture is to capitalize the local knowledge. It also follows the tradition of culture. Use of vernacular materials is also energy efficient rather than the using modern materials. Implementing ancient thoughts in modern technology helps to design. As per the view of Indian Architect Late Charles Correa," Vernacular Architecture has much things to teach as it always develops typology of fundamental sense". The Brick house at Wada, Mumbai is one of the most popular examples of using vernacular process with Modern Technology. Making of the brick house was an idea to use the material like bamboo, brick and others in their naked form. This fusion of vernacular and modern is not only eco-friendly and cost effective but also gives a contemporary look to the architecture.

The Krupachhaya farmhouse in Pune is other example of mix and match of modern and vernacular architecture. The use of local red stone, a spacious center hall and Wooden wall for thermal insulation is a lesson from vernacular technology to use in modern structures to meet the needs of people within the modern looks. Use of terracotta roofing and the glass opening is inspired from the old technology. The use of jali skin for filtering the air and the step walls to insulate the temperature in pearl houses of Rajasthan is an attractive example of fusion architecture. In modern days the early style of architecture is used to depict the history and the culture of the particular region and also to promote tourism. The resorts in Andaman are an example of Vincent culture to tourists which also has a great historical value in modern days.

Mud walls and the steep slanting roofs of Oland Estate in Tamil Nadu simply shows the influence of implementing vernacular Strategy to modern techniques. The structure of the roof is to protect the house from rain falling and to five the identity of a good example of ancient culture and modern techniques.

Research shows that 39% of Carbon Dioxide consumption is for construction work which is absolutely not eco-friendly. Modern materials like steel, glass do not contain enough thermal mass and for this reason these materials do not have the capability of holding and releasing the temperature. The result of this incapability is increasing the tendency to installing of Cooling materials in modern houses as temperatures are increasing day by day due to global warming and modern techniques of construction fail to act according to the temperature. All these hazards of modern techniques are also increasing the cost of living. So, the Architect are trying to implement the native ways to construct or to design the building.

Architect are focusing to use the local materials to lower the cos of transportation and increasing the availability of the resources. Reviving the original knowledge, taking climate consideration and flexibility into account, and organizing the space according to daily needs are critical issues. Low energy consumption levels were once easy to achieve without sacrificing comfort. The purpose of the study of vernacular construction is not to return to the past because it would be unbearable and possibly merely superficial imitation, but rather to gain knowledge of the criteria for house designing based on adaptable lifestyles. It is concluded from the research and the experience that implementing vernacular architecture to modern techniques are very important in terms of effective costing, ecofriendly, climate responsive houses and most importantly availability of local resources and knowledge.

Thus, understanding Vernacular Architecture and its characteristics are very important for architects, as it can help regulate the brimming problem of environmental degradation and also help society stay true to its culture and heritage. A proper approach has to be adapted in the induction of these vernacular values in architects, which has to begin at the grass-root level that is at the graduation level, following proper specializations. It has to be given more importance than just mugging up the definition, **only then will the results be visible.**

Acknowledgements

Writing a Book could be way harder than you think, but perhaps can be rewarding in ways more than you could ever imagine!

> *" "No one who achieves success does so without acknowledging the help of others." – Alfred North Whitehead "*

I have come to realize, the hard way, that having an idea and turning it into a book can be much more painstaking than it sounds. The experience can be both internally challenging as well as massively enriching. I believe that it's definitely about introspection, understanding our own internal locus of focus; and because a Book like this, in its true sense, becomes nothing less than an Architectural Project to me, so it's also probably a lot about teamwork in all its practicality and implementation.

When you feel extremely thankful for someone, translating your gratitude into words can be difficult. There is always, always, always something to be thankful for. I believe that saying thank you is more than just good manners, it is good spirituality, because gratitude can transform common days into thanksgiving, turn routine jobs into joy and change ordinary opportunities into blessings. I believe we must make it our habit to tell people thank you. To express our appreciation, sincerely and without the expectation of anything in return. If you truly appreciate life, you'll find that you have more of it.

Therefore, I especially want to thank the individuals and organizations who helped me to make my galactic endeavor, transpire to fruition.

"Gratitude is one of the least articulate of the emotions, especially when it is deep." – Felix Frankfurter, American Supreme Court Justice

Allow me to acknowledge the help and support of all the people involved in this uniquely positioned Industry-Academic interfacing Book/project, with the theme which is fondly called the THINK BEYOND ARCHITECTURE Series, of which this particular Book is named as "EVIDENCE BASED DESIGN APPROACH TO EXPLORE THE INDIAN VERNACULAR ARCHITECTURE", and, thanking more specifically, to the editors of this publication, who took the pain through the entire process.

Let me have the privilege to appreciate the overwhelming support received from the assisting Publication team of 'Mentordesk Academy' (https://www.facebook.com/mentordeskacademy/), a wholly owned subsidiary of the AskPEGASUS ADVISORY CONSULTANCY SERVICES OPC PRIVATE LIMITED, powered by the Chakrabarti Welfare Trust, operating from India since 1999. Mentordesk Academy had been a highly acclaimed academic mentoring, career counseling, coaching and employment supporting brand, working around the theme of 3E's - EDUCATION, EVALUATION & EMPLOYMENT, having regionally recognized for their continuous support towards the ongoing complete full-circle career requirements of candidates, while truly believing that tomorrow belongs to those who prepare for it today. I would wish to acknowledge the absolutely valuable contributions of the reviewers regarding the improvement of the overall quality, coherence, and content presentation. Without their support, this 'mega project' would not have become a reality.

Further, I would like to thank each one of the Technical contributors from across the Industry and Academics. Sincere gratitude goes to the Executives, Officials and the Administrators from various Departments of the State (West Bengal) Government as well as the Central Government of India, who contributed their time and expertise to enrich this project as a whole.

> *""When I started counting my blessings, my whole life turned around." —Willie Nelson"*

I should also take this opportunity to thank all the Government officials, Policy Makers, Researchers, Engineers, Environmentalists and Local Inhabitants of the 'New Town Kolkata Green Smart City', for their sincere help and support in my research project works.

I sincerely believe that this particular Book as part of its overall project intent, would not have been possible without those numerous multinational Corporate organizations and Governments Authorities, who facilitated me to develop and test insight-related ideas in projects, workshops, and consulting engagements over the past two decades.

The world becomes a better place, thanks to people I have interacted with, who wants to benevolently help and support others in their works. I believe what make it even better are people who share the gift of their time to mentor future leaders. Thanks to everyone who strives to grow and help others grow.

> *""Some people arrive and make such a beautiful impact on your life, you can barely remember what life was like without them." – Anna Taylor"*

Many thanks to my Parents, Mrs. Gouri Chakrabarti and Mr. Mani Sankar Chakrabarti, for supporting me throughout. And finally, last but not the least, I would definitely take this opportunity here to express a load of loving thanks to my Dearest Wife Suvalaxmi Chakrabarti and our Sweetest Little Daughter Chandrika Chakrabarti (AKA Saptami Chakrabarti), who missed me a lot during my lengthy and late research hours, during my strenuous and prolonged Online or Offline seminars and classes, or when I was away from home for academic or business tours for days or even months together, but they were phenomenally supportive and understanding, not only throughout the entire tenure of creating this Book and more, but also in order to fulfill our new normal life and family as a whole.

Much kind thanks to everyone living in and around My World!

Prologue

Let me tell you a story!

On the banks of the Chaliyar river, 12km away from Kozhikode in Kerala, is the home of an NRI couple who too parted with the concrete jungle for something closer to the real thing—a lush, 6-acre plot of land. What was meant to be a weekend home turned into a secluded escape for the family in the year of lockdowns and social-distancing.

The glass façade of this Kozhikode home reflects the dynamic scenery through the day. Photo: Syam Sreesylam/ Thought Parallels

The 2,220-square-foot glass-and-concrete structure, topped by a wing-shaped inverted roof of lightweight steel and wood, peeks out from this vegetation and quietly puts on a show. "Like a mirror, the structure reflects the sky, river, and greenery. Solar-reflective glazing creates a unique ocular experience: a façade that shape-shifts as day morphs into dusk," the architects explain.

In contrast to the façade, the material palette of concrete, kadappa tiles and wooden slats on the ceiling makes for interiors that are a nod to Kerala's vernacular architecture and feel cosy and lived-in. In the two bedrooms, on the first floor, the glass façade allows one to simultaneously revel in the feeling of lying outdoors under a canopy of trees and enjoy the creature comforts of a vintage wooden four-poster bed. The view remains the hero even in the powder room, which is fitted with a picture window that overlooks the river.

Vernacular Architecture has seen many such unique manifestations until this day. Vernacular Architecture constitutes 95% of the world's built environment, as estimated in 1995 by Amos Rapoport, as measured against the small percentage of new buildings every year designed by Architects and built by engineers.

"Vernacular Architecture constitutes 95% of the world's built environment."

Vernacular Architecture is broadly defined as an Architectural style which reflects local traditions. It is designed with indigenous construction material and based on the local needs. According to Ar. Kanika Dey Sarkar (Published in Indian Vernacular Planning) the term "vernacular" was initiated in 1800 as a concept and is derived from a Latin word vernaculus, meaning domestic, native and indigenous. In terms of architecture, it refers to an indigenous style specific to a place or time.

The Encyclopaedia of the Vernacular Architecture of the world defines Vernacular Architecture as consisting of the dwellings and all other buildings. It is related to their environmental contexts and available resources. They utilize traditional technologies. Vernacular Architecture is built to meet the specific needs, accommodating the values, economies, and ways of life of the cultures that produce them.

Frank Lloyd Wright describes Vernacular Architecture as

> *""Folk building growing in response to actual needs, fitted into an environment by people who knew no better than to fit them with native feeling.""*

Vernacular Architecture originated when people were forced to use natural resources as a shelter, in response to climate. It is a type of architecture which is native to a specific time and place and is not copied or replicated from anywhere, and uses handmade old construction practices. Furthermore, it emphasizes sustainability, and using materials which ensure that a structure stays cool from inside without the need of power intensive air-conditioning. In a nutshell, it includes the basic green architectural principles of energy efficiency and uses materials in the proximity of the site.

It is influenced by human behavior and the environment. Architects have been sourcing climate responsive methods which can be applied to modern construction. It is a result of four basic factors, namely:

1. *Site*

2. *Climate*
3. *Material*
4. *Skill*

One of the most significant influences on vernacular architecture is the macro climate of the area. The design of vernacular architecture evolves over time in sync with the context where the building exists and including various other factors like:

- **Availability of resources**
- **Skilled workforce**
- **Climatic and geological**
- **Historical influence**
- **Local culture**
- **Environment**
- **Natural and local skills**
- **Local technology**
- **Local materials**

The built environment of any community is considered to be the reflection of regional architecture – and thereby a significant component of differentiation.

In the pre-Industrial Revolution phase, India's built environment, as in the rest of the world, was shaped by certain values and cultural beliefs.

However, with tremendous urbanization and globalization after the Industrial Revolution, India's rich cultural and architectural heritage is vanishing. This is primarily due to increased usage of industrially-produced and standardized materials.

With that, the dependency on locally-available materials has declined, transforming 'vernacular architecture' buildings to more standardized modern concrete structures.

Vernacular architecture refers to structures built indigenous to a specific time or place, taking into consideration the experience of centuries of community building. It depicts the characteristics of the local environment, technology and climatic conditions.

Importantly, buildings constructed through traditional techniques using natural, locally-sourced, non-toxic, renewable and biodegradable materials can also minimize negative ecological impacts.

Modern architecture, on the other hand, uses industrially-produced materials (such as steel and concrete) that possess a low thermal resistance and require high energy intensity, thereby causing a considerable impact on the environment due to substantial energy consumption.

"Modern structures consume around 10 to 15% more energy compared to vernacular ones."

In Vernacular Architecture, users design and build at the same place. So, vernacular houses are more cost-effective as compared to contemporary-style houses. An affordable home design methodology is used to minimize cost and environmental impacts.

As Vernacular Architecture is all about using locally available materials for construction, the materials used in this architecture vary from place-to-place. But generally, the construction elements include adobe, rammed earth, mud bricks, thatch, cob, bamboo, stone, clay, timber, compressed brick blocks, clay-fly ash burnt bricks etc. It is sheltered in response to climate; culturally connects with the surroundings; and uses materials that are available locally.

Various vernacular practices have evolved over the years with locally available materials and new techniques to fulfil the needs of the people. Climate is the factor responsible for influencing the architectural forms and keeping the inhabitants comfortable. In a climate-response aspect, the building designs have incorporated various elements, like the interior courtyard – in order to escape the summer heat.

As quoted by the renowned Indian architect, the late Charles Correa,

> *"In this, the old Architecture – especially from vernacular – has much to teach us, as it always develops a typology of fundamental sense."*

In the modern world, vernacular strategies must be applied to modern Architecture, where the architectural design for homes is incorporated as a vernacular style in the contemporary forms. Many of the sustainable architecture and its design principles depend on the references to vernacular architecture.

Vernacular Architecture establishes a relationship between people, climate, and architecture. It demonstrates identity and sustainability, and I am on a Mission to teach the same to 1,000,000 Students of Architecture in order to make them employable for the industry, ready to fight the New Normal Post-Pandemic World out there, because Vernacular Architecture reflects time, place, and culture and the sustainable approach had already been existing in Vernacular Architecture forever since.

I fondly call it my 'Mission Million'!

Whether you are an unemployed Architect who has just lost your job, or are recently graduate or just finishing school, ideas in my Think Beyond Architecture Series of Books will help you find some immediate-action strategies to help make a living while also maintaining a designer's skill set for future work. Tactics include assembling a patchwork of part-time engagements that utilize Architectural skills, expanding a job search by pursuing remote work in distant locations, and starting to build a framework for your own little practice, in the most sustainable way for the future.

Check out for more: *https://www.facebook.com/ sschakrabarti.fanpage*

If you are studying to become an Architect or you are a practicing Architect, and you find these ideas resonate with yourself, this means that you are truly passionate about Architecture and genuinely care about your career.

"*"The pandemic reinforces what we already know."*
— *Bechara Choucair*"

Elements of sustainable design are integral to Vernacular Architecture that have evolved over time using local materials and technology emerging from ambient natural and cultural environment, creating optimum relationships between people and their place, and this is important, because difficult times are ahead of us.

Not a gloomy start for the aspiring Architects, but a word of caution:

Get ready to think, talk, look and live differently, only then can you sustain!

CHAPTER ONE

Indian Vernacular Architecture

India has rich vernacular traditions.

Indian Architecture presents a varied range of vernacular styles. The Indian vernacular style can be observed in different rural areas of the country, whereby structures are built with native materials designed to meet the needs of the local people. It has evolved gradually over time with the help of skilful craftsmanship. It is one of the most beautiful styles of architecture.

India, located on the Tropic of Cancer, boasts of a range of geographical and climatic conditions that each pose a unique set of challenges to a design. Every region has its own socio-cultural and topographic influence on architecture. These, along with historic traditions and availability of resources, have dictated how local techniques have evolved and been perfected over decades. As regional climate can vary from extreme snowfall to scorching desert heat, indigenous materials and vernacular practices play a huge role in shaping forms and functions.

Indian climate can be broadly classified into 5 zones:

1. *Hot and Arid*

2. *Warm and Humid*
3. *Temperate*
4. *Cold*
5. *Composite*

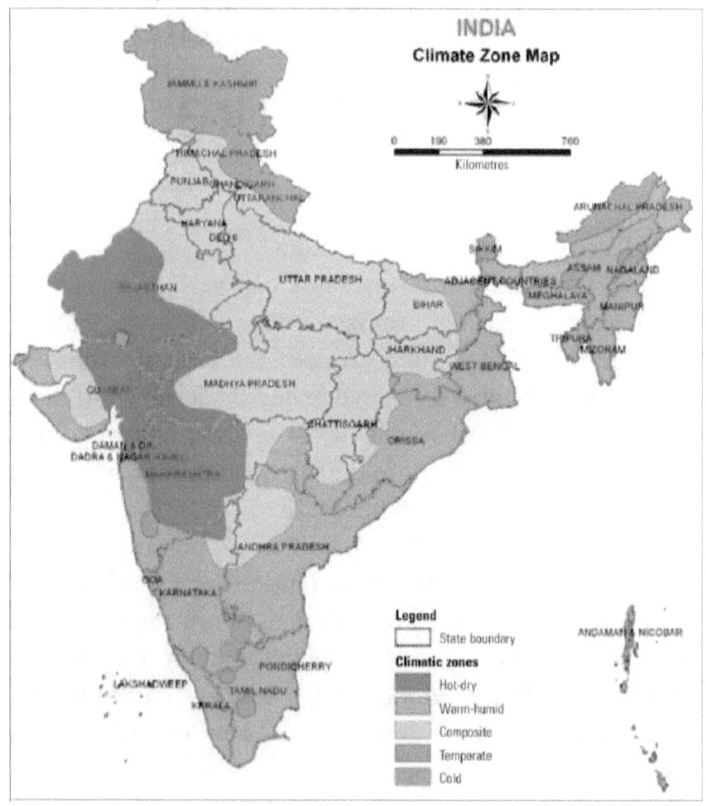

Climatic zones of India_©National Building Code of India, 2005

Architecture native to an area differs vastly from zone to zone, with the same material being used diversely in different climates. Recently, the architectural tone in the country has been of a revival of innovation in sustainable concepts; with growing awareness of ecologically responsible construction, architects are re-interpreting traditional methods in unique & unusual ways. If you're wondering how to adapt your design to its natural habitat, then read on to know some distinct features that will help you get the best out of your built space.

Hot and Arid Climate

- **Characterized by:** Sandy & rocky savannas, sparse vegetation, low humidity, high daytime temperatures, harsh sun, perennial hot & dusty winds, scarce water sources (Think desert).
- **Extending across:** Most of Rajasthan, parts of Gujarat & Maharashtra.
- **Best suited local construction materials:** Mud blocks, stone, and timber.

Local design & planning methods:

1. *Rooms placed around a central courtyard ensure good cross ventilation & natural cooling of interiors.*
2. *Using buffer spaces like corridors or storage spaces towards South and West faces shelters livable areas from maximum heat load.*
3. *Less street frontage minimizes surface heat gain.*
4. *Thicker walls made of earth bricks, which are poor conductors of heat, provide insulation from heat.*
5. *Window openings towards exterior faces should be smaller and of a lesser number. Instead, openings facing into the*

courtyard work better.

6. *Windows shaded with Chajjas (sunshades) or Jharokhas (intricately detailed stone bay windows) prevent direct sunlight from heating interior surfaces.*

7. *Ventilators at higher levels allow hot upper air to escape.*

8. *Jalis (latticework or screens) in semi-open areas like balconies and passages block heat while allowing light and air to filter in.*

9. *Flat roofs finished with white broken tiles reflect heat and at the same time offer ample surface area for ancillary terrace activities. It is common to sleep on Charpais (a local bed made of light materials) placed on the terrace or balconies at night.*

10. *Water bodies & greenery in and around the building are excellent solutions for passive cooling.*

11. *Exterior surfaces of the building are painted in light colors that reflect light. Dark colors are avoided due to their absorbent nature.*

12. *Neighborhood buildings benefit from being closely packed as they can shade each other.*

Warm and Humid Climate

- **Characterized by:** High humidity & rainfall, warm temperature, dense vegetation, moist winds at low speeds, diffused glare from the sun, hurricane or cyclone-prone (Think coastal regions).
- **Extending across:** Kerala, Tamil Nadu, Goa and parts of Karnataka, Odisha, Andhra Pradesh, West Bengal & North-Eastern India.

- **Best suited local construction materials:** Laterite stone or mud blocks, granite, timber, thatch or coconut leaves, bamboo, and Mangalore tiles.

Local design & planning methods:

1. *Similar to hot areas, courtyards are integral in providing relief from humidity as they allow the breeze to cross-ventilate inner spaces well. While central courts are common in Kerala or Chettinad homes, houses in Assam are raised on stilts to catch cool air and also protect against natural disasters that are common in these regions.*
2. *Rooms are placed in a line to ventilate them from two sides & accessed through corridors.*
3. *Kitchens & bathrooms are usually separated from main living areas with buffer passages as they generate more heat.*
4. *Shaded verandahs (entrance porches) & breezy porticos offer perfect daytime habitation potential.*
5. *While window openings being more in number & large in sizes let cool air in, they need extended shading devices that protect from the sun's glare.*
6. *Pitched Mangalore tile or thatch roofing supported on bamboo or timber framework allows rain to runoff conveniently or be directed into wells/ ground pits that harness the water. Overhanging eaves that extend well beyond walls shade from maximum heat.*
7. *Latticed or louvered window shutters protect from the harsh sun while allowing air to pass through.*
8. *Local stone or oxide floors are cost-effective and reduce the indoor temperature.*
9. *External surfaces are painted white to reflect heat.*

10. *Due to lush landscape growth, insects and critters are common; bug mesh in window & door frames are a good solution to tackle them.*

Cold Climate

- **Characterized by:** High altitude, low temperature, dense vegetation, brittle & direct sunlight, occasional strong winds, seasonal rain or snowfall depending on the altitude (Think mountains & hill stations).
- **Extending across:** Ladakh, Kashmir, Sikkim, parts of Arunachal Pradesh, Himachal Pradesh & Uttaranchal, and few hill stations in West & South India.
- **Best suited local construction materials:** Stone, mud, timber, thatch or slate, and mud or cow dung plaster.

Local design & planning methods:

1. *Buildings are generally 2-3 stories high, with most habitable rooms faced towards South & West to receive maximum sunlight.*
2. *Lower floors can be used for cattle, poultry, storage, etc while the upper floors consist of living spaces like kitchen, dining, etc due to the above floors being warmer. Minimal partitions between rooms keep heat uniform on the entire floor.*
3. *Thick walls made of local stone or mud are plastered in multiple layers to insulate against the cold and trap heat indoors.*
4. *Openings are majorly found on the South with other walls protecting from cold draughts.*

5. *Pitched roofs of timber/ bamboo frames, finished with slate or thatch prohibit rain or snow from collecting on the roof. Attics formed below the pitched roof are well insulated against the cold.*
6. *Only in the cold & arid weather of Ladakh, flat roofs are used as the probability of rainfall is less and this space can be used for drying fruits & vegetables in summer.*
7. *Wooden floors keep the floor cozy.*
8. *Strategically planted tall trees can act as windbreakers.*
9. *Timber balconies act as solariums.*
10. *Due to the rugged appearance of the surroundings, vibrant colors in elements such as windows or columns add a welcome detail.*

Temperate & Composite Climates

The only 2 cities of India having temperate (comfortable temperature throughout the year) would be Pune & Bangalore. The vernacular of these regions imitate their neighboring coastal towns, with the courtyard becoming the prominent feature around which other spaces revolve. With architecture seeing swift modernization, contemporary concrete buildings are replacing traditional Wada & Gutthu houses.

Most Central Indian states experience a composite of hot-dry and warm-humid climates with few months of each. Their architecture features elements taken from both regions, like courtyards, large overhangs, water bodies, landscaping, neutral colors, etc., that focus on withstanding heat as well as rain. Built from locally available materials & resources, these showcase the versatility of Indian vernacular that has withstood the test of time and continues to reflect in some form in the contemporary buildings being designed even today.

Sustainable Indian Architecture Techniques and Elements

Our history has a significant impact on developing our lives. The historic technologies that our forefathers used are exceptionally iconic. There has been an environmental balance maintained between the human and natural environments in the early periods. They believed in intertwining nature and architecture to create a spectacular scene that did not detract from the natural features of the surrounding. Natural integration has long been a feature of all ancient cultures, including India. This is evident in the numerous religious, social, and ancient traditions, ceremonies, art and sculpture, and folk stories that prevail in multiple forms in Indians' everyday life.

1. Arches

Indian architectural style has used both false and true arches, although structural arches seem to be notably absent from Hindu temple architecture throughout all times. Arches are enchanting design elements that are rarely seen in modern homes. Arches have a great charm to them because of their smooth curves, which are a nice departure from straight lines and right angles. They have the added benefit of being structurally stable due to their design. This implies that they can be built without the use of a lintel, which is typically utilized to support all door and window openings. Arches can be built out of bricks or stone, reducing the quantity of concrete needed for the lintels. In corridors and verandahs, arches are particularly charming.

2. Wind Catchers

Hyderabad's unusual skyline, occupied by wind-catchers, was once its most notable feature. These wind catchers, or Manghu in Sindhi, were installed on housetops to capture the south-westerly wind during the sunny days and evening hours. They consisted of a tower opening with a scoop on their upper end that directed the wind inside the house. This ancient Indian technique can lower the temperature and supply fresh air to building users while also lowering CO_2 concentrations.

3. Courtyard

Ancient Indian architecture is credited with building pleasant indoor environments through the use of strategic natural ventilation. Courtyards are built into several traditional dwellings in India. This is partly because of the Indian courtyard's adaptability and ability to perform numerous wonders. It works as a heat sink, promotes evaporative cooling, and allows for c

ross ventilation. It is transformed into a meeting place for celebrations. It becomes a location for secondary culinary tasks such as drying pickles and grinding spices. It becomes a gathering place for ladies to sit and talk. It is occasionally used for gardening, while other times it is used to keep cattle.

4. Verandah

A verandah is a lengthy raised area that spans more than one of a house's exterior walls and is usually used for outdoor activities. It is a transitory space that integrates the interior and exterior, removing the abrupt and harsh shift from the openness of the exterior world to the closed interior spaces. This helps the breeze spill in through the veranda flowing freely through the living areas. A naturally cool house does not require environmentally unfriendly cooling methodologies, making a veranda a rather sustainable alternative.

5. Built-in Furniture

Some furniture in traditional Indian architecture was built while the house was being built. The front verandah in several Kerala and Goan homes used to have built-in seating. Moreover, they also housed niches, alcoves, and shelves for storage, displays, and lanterns. The built-in furniture was extremely durable and also helped to save money on woodwork.

Let's have a look at some interesting aspects of Indian Vernacular Architecture:

There are different kinds of Vernacular Architecture in India in its different Regions. A few of the different types of Indian Vernacular Architecture Style are described below.

1.Koti Banal from uttarkashi District of Uttarakhand.

This 900 years old construction is mainly planned to resist the effect of earthquake in hilly areas.It is a Two to three storey building made of bamboo and the support of wooden logs. These type of building has minimal number of openings to trap the heat in the house.

This type of multi Storey building is made to keep the cattle in the first storey and the second or third storey is for the owner and for the belongings.

2.Bhunga from Kutch district of Gujarat.

In this type of architectural form the room is shaped in cylinder form and the wooden supported roof is shaped in a conical form.This cylinder type house contains a single room with a door and windows.This type of house demands regular maintenance as it protects from the high velocity desert winds and heat of the desert.

3.Bamboo House of Assam.

This typical traditional house of Assam is made to resist the effect of flood of a particular area of Assam.The house is made of timber frame and Ikra and the wall is coated with mud plating.The structure is made for two storeyed buildings.The roof-top of this house is downward slope to overcome the waterlogging of heavy raining.The local grass is used to made the roof-top is changeable after 10 years.

4.Mud and Timber Architecture of Ladakh.

Base of this type of house is made of lime to absorb the water easily and the wall of the house consists of easily available and cheap mud brick. The walls are usually thick to avoid the structural damages due to earthquakes. Due to dry and cold weather mud and wood are used to insulate the properties and the height of the ceiling are kept comparatively low to trap the heat. This type of house is required to be maintained every year.

5.Chuttillu from Visakhapatnam District of Andhra Pradesh.

This Architectural form found in the coastal area of South India. It is shaped like a traditional hut and it has Two or three rooms.The middle room is used to store the crops during summer and in winter time it is used as a sleeping area. This inner room is circled with another room. The roof top is made up of the leaves of the local trees.

The traditional form of Architecture varies in different regions of India and it changes with the time period. The purpose of the Architecture form is to serve on an immediate basis and to mitigate the local needs.So the materials used for the construction also depend on the particular regions.Thus the construction style in Vernacular Architecture reflects the traditional art of a particular region.

The vernacular is the informal style of architecture and this informal style does not need any bookish idea to construct the building rather it depends on the skill of local craft man. The main purpose of the architecture is to build sustainable solutions for the local people. As it is a solution for local people and India has various climate areas throughout the country, the Architecture has its own story in the different regions.

Why Should The Student's Of Architecture Study Vernacular Architecture?

Why should the students really study any aspect of Architecture? Well, Architecture for sure is an interesting and sophisticated subject but who really knows what it means. For many people it still is just making buildings. But the interested people know, so for them and for people who don't already know let's talk something more about Vernacular Architecture.

Vernacular Architecture refers to the construction which is made using local or traditional materials which is usually collected from the area near the construction. According to its etymology, "verna" means native and "architecture" is to design buildings, thus Vernacular Architecture is an architecture style that is built to meet the present needs, keeping in mind the local climate, culture, and materials. They are placed in geographically correct areas which are also rich in its culture and heritage. Due to its unique features, the correct definition of vernacular architecture was not clear until author, Paul Oliver redefined the term in his book "Built to Meet Needs: Cultural Issues in Vernacular Architecture (2006)" that, it is an architecture that encompasses the peoples' dwellings and other constructions, relating to their respective environments and resources, usually built by the owners or the community, using traditional techniques. It is built to meet specific needs, accommodate the values, economy, and lifestyles of a specific culture.

Before 1800's, the term Vernacular was looked down upon and was used for an entity that was considered ordinary, basic and designed out of necessity. The Vernacular Architecture design is based on availability of workforce, local technology,climate,local culture (which includes the number of family members, social condition, local customs etc.), environment , economic conditions and also historical influences.

There are many benefits of learning about vernacular architecture for the students from the architectural background.

- *Understanding traditions and local culture of the place.*
- *Efficient usage of the raw materials and the local resources which makes the energy sufficient and sustainable.*
- *Creating connection between humans and the natural habitat.*

As Frank Lloyd Wright says, "Architects cannot or should not create spaces without their connections with the historical roots". Vernacular Architecture is sustainable compared to modern architecture. Considering the example of the Warli House in Maharashtra, they use special stones called Karvi Stones to create a light exterior that diminishes the external heat creating a cool atmosphere inside amidst the hot and humid climate of Maharashtra.

India is a land full of culture. There are many examples of such Vernacular Architecture like Havelis of Ahmedabad, Houses of Himachal Pradesh,etc.The relevance of studying this type of architecture is to preserve the cultural heritage of our country. The narrow street designs, the brick architecture, grain storage rooms and much more are slowly fading away due to the onset of modern design and architecture.

A proper approach to adapt vernacular values in architecture helps to preserve such beautiful architectures. Importance to learning this type of vernacular architecture can help us bring back the history and culture while making the architecture more environmentally friendly and the designs more sustainable for the future generations by **using the local materials and resources of our country raher than using the imported foreign materials.**

The Father of Modern Vernacular Architecture In India

Lawrence Wilfred "Laurie" Baker (2 March 1917 – 1 April 2007) was a British-born Indian architect, renowned for his initiatives in cost-effective energy-efficient architecture and designs that maximized space, ventilation, and light and maintained an uncluttered yet striking aesthetic sensibility. Influenced by Mahatma Gandhi and his own experiences in the remote Himalayas, he promoted the revival of regional building practices and use of local materials; and combined this with a design philosophy that emphasized a responsible and prudent use of resources and energy.

Lawrence Wilfred "Laurie" Baker (2 March 1917 – 1 April 2007)

He was a pioneer of sustainable architecture as well as organic architecture, incorporating in his designs even in the late 1960s, concepts such as rain-water harvesting, minimizing usage of energy-inefficient building materials, minimizing damage to the building site and seamlessly merging with the surroundings. Due to his social and humanitarian efforts to bring architecture and design to the common man, his honest use of materials, his belief in simplicity in design and in life, and his staunch Quaker belief in non-violence, he has been called the "Gandhi of architecture".

His work reflects the same and inspires us to incorporate and build unique, personal structures among the ocean of highly commercialized, look-alike buildings with no personality.

Baker believed that the building to be designed derives its personality from the clients who use it.

""You will be putting up their building, not yours",*
he often told his students."

He stressed the use of "Common Sense", while designing which emphasizes avoiding the excess and the extravagance. The duty of an architect is to accept a brief that he is capable of performing while encouraging his client to renounce that which is not necessary. As an architect, we must research and study our site, its advantages, and its shortcomings, and make the most we can in an honest and efficient manner. His philosophies of cost-effective, energy-efficient designs using indigenous materials were assimilated through the various experiences that taught him the importance of these aspects.

Born into a strict Christian Methodist family, Laurie spent his early days devoted to the church and all its activities. His interest in the traditional church teachings reduced during the teen years and he was introduced to Quaker beliefs, very similar to the teachings of Mahatma Gandhi. It was Gandhi who said that ideal houses in the ideal village will be built using materials which are all found within a 5-mile radius of the house and it is this principle Laurie incorporated in all his projects. His affinity to Gandhi's teachings is what gave him the title that he is known for now.

After a 4 year stint in China volunteering in a medical camp, Laurie returned to England only to move to India in 1945 to build hospitals that could treat leprosy patients. He was finally ready to use his architectural skills to help the people in need.

Despite being a RIBA qualified architect, he faced unexpected obstacles. Inspecting and building new structures in the remote areas of India meant having the knowledge of local materials like Laterite, mud, and cow dung building construction techniques and dealing with problems like torrential rain, termites, and even Bed bugs.

Learning about the local materials and its building techniques to use them in a manner that would please his clients and also fit into the local styles was the emergence of what we call now as the "Laurie Baker Architecture".

During his days in Pithoragarh, he learned that dealing with real-world problems like poverty was essential while designing, and learning to build inexpensively was the way to coping with housing needs in a world where people lived in extreme dearth. His principles of cost efficiency, conscious designing, and durability in structures have been integrated after serving the people living on these Himalayan foothills. "Small is not only beautiful but is often essential and more important than Large" is an important characteristic of Baker Architecture.

His final stop in Kerala showcases his maximum work in Architecture. With his principles set and his acquired local knowledge to support his beliefs, Laurie Baker set out to build more than 1000 residences, 40 churches, and other institutional buildings during his stay in Trivandrum. The famous brickwork construction that has become the trademark of Baker architecture was developed while solving the problem of low-cost building techniques during this era. "Bricks to me are like faces", a quote that intrigues us while learning about this material came from the creator of the 'Rat Trap Bond'. Keeping the materials in its raw state was essential for him and building unique patterns with the natural texture it provides is what brings out the character in each of his buildings.

Most people associate Laurie Baker Architecture with Brick construction but Laurie rightfully points out that, it is only his most recent and known buildings in Kerala that have bricks as its primary building material. Baker Style is not specific to one single material but various indigenous materials based on its Building location. Baker style in Uttar Pradesh, Gujarat, and West Bengal all vary as per their location but their core philosophy remains the same.

The Hamlet

Laurie Baker's residence situated along the slope of a rocky hill in Trivandrum is a unique house suited to his family's needs and way of life. It consisted of a living room, bedroom, library, and kitchen, all built using the traditional brick and timber resources. Rooms were modest and equipped with maximum natural ventilation achieved due to an open room design, jaali walls, gables, tilted, and louvered windows. Discarded colored bottles were used as decoration to give a stained glass effect, Mangalore tiles on the roof as per the vernacular style and bits and pieces of metal to create beautiful grill patterns. The site as Laurie insisted on all his works would be modified to the minimum. The building was designed around the trees and steps leading to his house were cut into the rocks existing in its path. Even the door of his house was created by using traditional doors discarded from a building that was initially torn down. His house embodies his legacy and defines what he truly believes in.

The Centre of Development Studies, Trivandrum

This 10-acre campus situated on the outskirts of Trivandrum in a residential area is one of Baker's most noted designs. A Library and computer center, Auditoriums, Hostels, and residential quarters for staff, this green campus is also noted for its famous garden.

Buildings were designed to suit the contoured land and molded around the trees that obstructed its path. This created interesting wall shapes and spaces that accommodate courtyards and pools that not only added to the aesthetics about also temperature control. Roofs of various shapes with openings towards the wind direction acted as gables. Baker's trademark brick jali, filler slab roof of Mangalore tiles and exposed material was evident on this campus. Granite aggregates in the shape of flowers and leaves can be seen in the concrete pavements outside, which reflected the mason's creativity that Baker encouraged during the building process.

Careful consideration and techniques like double walls and perforated brick jaalis were incorporated to achieve climate control and create comfortable spaces within the building at all times to achieve an efficient and ideal campus.

Laurie Baker's legacy now lives through his Center for Habitat studies, located in Kerala. The various Programs and Summer schools organized his teachings and encouraged his sustainable style of Architecture. In an era where Nature itself rebels against the atrocities that have prevailed partly due to building construction techniques, we realize the importance of Laurie Baker's sustainable approach for a secure and comfortable future.

Sustainable, Organic, and Vernacular Architecture all synonymous to one of the greatest pioneers of this style, Lawrence Wilfred Baker, a British-born Architect. Also known as the Gandhi of Architecture, he reminds us that the true meaning of Architecture lies in the responsible and prudent use of limited resources and imbibing the characteristics that surround it.

Integrating Modern And Vernacular Architecture In Contemporary Designs

With the escalating ecological crisis across the world, there is a mounting threat to traditional and cultural values. Unplanned development that disregards local beliefs, culture and values have led to a widespread socio-economic imbalance. To make our communities more sustainable, vernacular elements need to be incorporated into contemporary town or city planning.

Various initiatives are being taken by Earth Summit, National Habitat Mission, JNNURM, Water mission and Energy Efficiency mission to create culturally supportive communities. After all, vernacular traditions enhance not only social inclusion but also citizens' quality of life.

Already, we are seeing an increasing focus on harvesting rainwater, and preserving and promoting recycling and reuse.

However, despite the challenges such as the provision of the built fabric in relation to the surrounding urban form, emphasis must also be given on building sustainable structures in response to the respective climatic conditions – structures which are energy-efficient and use natural, renewable materials such as mud and timber.

Visualizing the building as a completed dynamic state with the clients utilizing it, is the ultimate goal of an Architect. We can compare our Architectural profession to that of a Musical conductor, who controls all the musical instruments in his orchestra and has an overall view of how it sounds together to create the perfect symphony. This makes much sense when, as an Architect, I realize that it is my responsibility to coordinate and supervise all the technical aspects of building construction to achieve the perfect composition for my clients.

The question remains – what is your takeaway from this, as a budding Architect?

CHAPTER THREE

Evidence Based Design (EBD)

Nightmares are quickly becoming reality!

More than half the world's population already lives in urban centers, and in two decades that number will be more than 60 per cent. By 2039, our world will be home to at least 43 megacities—urban areas with more than 10 million inhabitants (UN, 2018).

> *"The question which is haunting us day and night is that how will the Smart Cities of the future deal with such an influx of people?"*

I believe the answer lies in the ethical implementation of Evidence Based Design (EBD) methodology in Urban Architecture.

Evidence Based Design (EBD) is the process of conceiving a building or physical environment based on scientific research methodology, in order to achieve the best possible outcomes.

The Center for Health Design (CHD) defines EBD as:

""the deliberate attempt to base building decisions on the best available research evidence with the goal of improving outcomes and of continuing to monitor the success or failure for subsequent decision-making.""

An evidence-based model can be used for all design decisions. Traditionally associated with Healthcare Architecture, Evidence Based Design (EBD) is making inroads into being part of the process for designing schools, office spaces, hotels, restaurants, museums, prisons and even residences. In short, EBD is when decisions about physical space are based on research and data.

An Architectural design solution is only as good as the quality of its Research.

Evidence-based design is an approach in which qualitative and quantitative research inform decisions. Evidence-Based Design approach is all about understanding how designers should conduct research into commercial or residential or other spaces and use this research to achieve optimal Architectural design solutions.

Evidence can be a powerful tool used to inform an Architects' decisions. Evidence Based Design (EBD) should therefore be very much a part of the mainstream process for designing schools, office spaces, hotels, restaurants, museums, prisons and even residences. In short, EBD is when decisions about physical space are based on real life due diligence and Research.

Evidence Based Design (EBD) is mostly about learning from others mistakes, and quickly shortcutting to the outcome without going through the entire iterative process of failures.

> *""Learn from the mistakes of others; you can't live long enough to make them all yourselves!!" - Acharya Chanakya"*

There are four components to evidence-based design:

1. **Gather qualitative and quantitative intelligence**
2. **Map strategic, cultural and research goals**
3. **Hypothesize outcomes, innovate, and implement translational design**
4. **Measure and share outcomes**

Through my personal experience of practicing and preaching for the past two decades, I have seen very closely that the practice of Architecture has adapted in response to some innovation, from new building materials to 2D and 3D Computer Aided Design & Drafting (CADD) and parametric design processes, but its core pedagogical theories remain parked in the past, often neglecting significant intelligent insights.

> *""We shape our buildings thereafter they shape us""*

This is a well-known quote by British Prime Minister Winston Churchill, in October 1943 regarding plans to rebuild the bomb-shattered House of Parliament. They do indeed shape us, Aarchitecture is the process of planning, designing and constructing but the physical structures of a building can have a significant influence on a person's mood and their overall perceptions of their surroundings. A building is an interaction between the eye and the brain and the environment that people live and work in has a huge effect on how they behave – human Psychology is directly related with Architecture.

Today, Scientists have come up with absolute evidence that the built environment affects humans, both mentally and physically. We can track it. We can deliver hard data and measure how different built environments affect biochemical changes in our bodies and can harm human health, both mentally and physically. This means we can no longer teach future Architects that the abstract parti is the unique central organizing feature of design; we need to add on something more, we need to put people and biology and human functions at the center of their thinking, just like top tech and automobile designers already do.

As Architectural design educators, we need to overcome the old premise of our core thinking, we need to understand that the humans enter the world hardwired to respond to specific patterns in very specific ways; carmakers and advertisers and computer scientists all know this, it's time for architects to learn biological reality, too.

> *"Understanding human psychology is absolutely essential for the Architects of the future."*

Scientists have since long argued that applied psychology methods can be used to understand how people respond to different designs before a building is built, thereby empowering the Architect to make improvements. But this research-based design approach has been largely dismissed by the mainstream Architectural education community, with the argument that at the heart of much of the environmental design literatures are studies that are subjective in nature, hard to replicate, or with limited internal validity. However, these limitations no longer hold us back. Today, the explosion of scientific and technological innovation has produced an array of new biometric tools for uncovering the thoughts, feelings, and emotional responses of people. This evidence can no longer be ignored by mainstream Architectural educators.

Architects, engineers, and urban planners of today should be thinking about the cities of tomorrow. First and foremost, our future cities must be places designed for people, not vehicles, buildings, and businesses.

Explaining and reviewing the processes of ethical implementation of Evidence Based Design (EBD) methodology in Urban Architecture is pivotal to the success of the students for the future.

I strongly believe that creating vibrant communities, connections, and relevance between people and place is paramount in an Urban Architectural construct. In the broadest sense, Urban Architecture is any building that has a perceptible relationship to other buildings at a pedestrian scale. In the most common sense, Urban Architecture is comprised of buildings located in towns or cities, regardless of use or size, where walking is a reasonable mode of transportation. This captures the whole range of scales between small rural villages and the largest metropolitan cities. It excludes suburban development patterns, which prioritize automobile transportation, usually at the expense of other forms like NMT. However, this is a continuum and not a polarity. The primary use of buildings in Urban Architecture is less important than the building form. Building uses change over time and good Urban Architecture is adaptable to cultural, societal and technological changes.

In my opinion, the following five major essentials will be absolutely critical to understand for the success of a smart city of the future, achieved by Evidence Based Design (EBD).

HUMAN-CENTRIC URBAN PLANNING

To create flourishing cities of the future, Architects and Urban Planners would have to address issues like public health and community building. Creating vibrant downtown districts, mixed-use spaces, human-powered and intermodal transit systems, and implementation of green spaces are all critical to this goal, by Design.

SMART TRANSPORTATION

Efficient Smart Transportation would free up street space formerly used by human drivers, creating open space for commerce, fitness, and relaxation. Such radical pedestrian-centric streetscape would prioritize sidewalks and bike lanes over cars and encourage more outdoor time in the lap of nature, by Design.

HIGH - RISE HIGH - PERFORMANCE BUILDINGS

In order to accommodate the skyrocketing population and preserve open spaces at the same time, High-rise High-performance superstructures would have to be conceived, which would be way taller than what we see today. Technologies such as ropeless elevators, which can move up, down, and side to side, shall enable unprecedented possibilities in the Architecture and design of buildings. Furthermore, buildings will promote healthier living, bringing in natural light deep into buildings, keeping humans in touch with our natural rhythms, by Design.

CLEAN AND GREEN ENERGY

Buildings are one of the biggest consumers of energy worldwide. Therefore ideally they should have their own decentralized, renewably generated clean and green energy generating plants. Using high-performance façades, photovoltaic panels, and geothermal and wind energy, buildings would generate their own energy, while smart technology and the smart grid would help them share it super efficiently. Energy would soon be harvested from every surface we use, to charge the whole city, achieved by Design.

CHANGE, CLIMATE CHANGE

We should be able to mitigate some of the effects of climate change. For coastal cities like Mumbai, infrastructure would have to be rethought as sea level rise changes the coastline and permeates the aquifer. Canals, bridges, and offshore solutions can help reinforce resilience, but all stakeholders must ask what assets they are willing to preserve, adapt, or lose for the greater good. Other cities, such as Delhi, would likely suffer serious drought. In these areas, capturing water from permeable surfaces and collecting and purifying storm water runoff, would be absolutely critical to achieve.

Maintaining a strong connection with the natural world would become increasingly critical, as our day-to-day activities would become increasingly tied to engagement with digital interfaces. Juxtaposing green spaces wherever possible, creating micro-parks, green balconies, green roofs, and vertical gardening would be on the rise. Natural elements such as parks, green roofs, wetlands, and bioswales should be used more and more in combating extreme weather events and the effects of climate change, by Design.

For mankind to preserve the planet's ecological health, we must change our perception of what our homes and industrial buildings should look like, and blend these with nature, rather than replacing nature with concrete. Architects need to make buildings more green and adaptable to our surroundings. They need to avoid the Sick Building Syndrome (SBS) and create buildings that are energy efficient.

Green design should be everywhere but there is a long way to go before it is the customary way of doing business. Many times economics and environmental aspects of a building tend to conflict with each other, as one is exchanged for the other. Architects need to design ecosystems to be healthier and lessen the pollution impact on the earth.

Architects today face a unique opportunity to reshape the environment so it's a better fit with our biological nature. They are in an unprecedented position to use evidence-based design and build what people want to, unconsciously, see and be in. With new biometric tools, they can more easily do post occupancy evaluations, asking people where they feel at their best, ensuring that new projects are successful by Design.

Evidence Based Design (EBD) is therefore not just reserved for Healthcare Architecture; but it applies to the entire Architectural domain in general, in creating healthful built environments for us all.

Evidence Based Design (EBD) is making major strides is in green design, because there's a clear connection between sustainable design and the need to collect evidence. There is a rapidly growing body of performance data on mechanical systems, lighting, building orientation, water and energy usage, and indoor air quality. Often the results show links between these things and the well being of facility users. This trend will continue as manufacturers of green materials invest heavily in research, as more clients seek IGBC or LEED certifications.

In the modern world, vernacular strategies must be applied to modern architecture where the architectural design for homes is incorporated as a vernacular style in the contemporary forms. Many of the sustainable architecture and its design principles depend on the references to vernacular architecture.

As vernacular architecture is all about using locally available materials for construction, the materials used in this architecture vary from place-to-place. But generally, the construction elements include adobe, rammed earth, mud bricks, thatch, cob, bamboo, stone, clay, timber, compressed brick blocks, clay-fly ash burnt bricks etc. It is sheltered in response to climate; culturally connects with the surroundings; and uses materials that are available locally.

Various vernacular practices have evolved over the years with locally available materials and new techniques to fulfil the needs of the people. Climate is the factor responsible for influencing the architectural forms and keeping the inhabitants comfortable. In a climate-response aspect, the building designs have incorporated various elements like the interior courtyard – in order to escape the summer heat.

Think Beyond Architecture.

As construction costs rise, codes increase and human-centered considerations flourish, clients will demand accountability and data-proven justification for most design decisions.

Architects, in their effort to remain both competitive and innovative, would likely seek strategies that allow their expertise to shine. Technology will improve the ease and availability of existing research, and will improve digital user-feedback and data gathering systems. No doubt it will be a group effort, a clear case of team work. No loner a 'lonely genius' Architect, an 'Alien' in isolation, shall be able to express justice to this enormous endeavor.

Evidence Based Design (EBD) must have to be embraced by our whole profession and those who seek our professional services in the not so far away in the future.

I am confident that eventually all mainstream Architects would surely open up their mind's window, and embrace an Evidence Based Design (EBD) Approach to Urban Architecture for the future.

CHAPTER FOUR

N – North

Vernacular Architecture of the North:

India is an enormous and compound nation with a varied culture serene of spiritual, topographical, cultural, climatic and verbal assortment. Its history is occupied by intense governmental, progressive and ethnic practices. It is a land-living of townships, but over a wide-ranging antiquity of suburbanization.

Today's language and outmoded Indian construction, consequently, have numerous indexes in covered manufactured environments. The inaccessible homesteads of Goa, the articulate woody architecture of Kerala, mountain residences of Himachal Pradesh, stilt-raised households of the North-East, the paddles of Maharashtra, pol firms and Havelis Gujarat, and the environmental incentive structure of Rajasthan validate the nation's local assortment.

Vernacular Architecture of the North

India can be around, separated into the individualities that lie to the north and the south of the Tropic of Cancer. Though the Indian topography, values, and common edifices change mostly amongst these dual sections, the archaeologist has to be situated commonly separating India as North and South India. It is apparent that practically the whole lot from the climatic environments to the possessions obtainable is dissimilar amongst these two portions of the nation. Consequently, the method that which persons respond to their instantaneous atmosphere is similarly actual diverse.

The apprehension for the weather as healthy as financial and cultural sustainability has remained observed in the latter two periods, lacking which sustainability organizes not exertion in the Indian background or somewhat indigenous background for that material.

Founded on this philosophy, "Aaranya", a cultivation farm stay, is positioned in pastoral environs at the advantage of Sasan Gir Lion Sanctuary, Gujarat. It remained considered by Ahmedabad-based enterprise workshop who exertion with a piercing attitude of vernacular style in their developments. Gujarat's existence a warm and thirsty climatic province, the and lodges have to be situated preoccupied within instruction to minimize warmth improvement and take full advantage of cross exposure to air.

The hip-roofing coordination that is instinctive to this constituency has been located instigated in the small house to counterpoise rainwater in heavy rain and heat in the summer. The undergrowth that requires to be been embedded on more than a few of the alternative's constructions not solitary assistance with temperature directive but when entirely grownup will assist the construction combination into its commonplace background.

Vernacular Architecture of the North

Grownup building methods consuming wreckage pebble crowded underpinning, load method unprotected natural stonework walls, element dome with china assortment on highest and earth earthen cemented rooftop are not only price tag operative and period verified, but also produce employ for the residents.

The Firodiya Center for Stimulus parks as a buildup of vernacular architectural familiarity both theoretically and chronologically. The expansion obligatory the formation of a managerial workplace space & educational colonnade for companies protected visually and acoustically after the manufacturing atmosphere from place to place.

Centred on hardheaded and conservational requirements, the draftswomen progressed the form bearing in mind the 15-year longstanding geodesic ceiling accommodated in the locations. This development purposes to generate an extremely maintainable property through the request of frequent approaches like a markdown of left-over peer group by reprocessing shaped waste.

90% of the construction usage construction is quantifiable and goods are accessible nearby. There is a sensitive operation of expected light-consuming skylights, north illumination and energy-efficient floor lamp. The outside display planetary is produced by astonishing fortifications in a method that the outside walkway can be secondhand through the daytime. External battlements are coloured in tinted rough surface, mixture with the usual and nearby. In pretentious difference, hearts are painted in flawless white with normal light.

The chocolate Kota shingle secondhand carpeting not only delivers a quiet self-possession to the interplanetary but likewise assists in possession of the floor's cool. Stumpy, enormous and with fluctuating dimensions, the construction is brashly fashionable but stimulated by its situation.

Studio Advaita henceforward planned this superb working out centre which can be understood as the eventual vernacular explanation for the farming communal. It was considered to be interstellar wherever the undeveloped cohort could acquire and appear various developments, although also present a material centre of agriculture for the close communities.

The Center will likewise be a demonstration planetary for scholars' exploration. The elementary strategy originates from native assemblies in and from place to place in Ahmednagar and the construction capitals are nominated prudently to assist monetary and architectural sustainability. Steely and dyed soar ash blocks are cast off with hollows for temperature wadding for the structure of exterior fortifications. Altogether inside spaces are requiring ordinary secondary sunny to diminish the feasting of power.

Vernacular Architecture of the North

The Kondan Retreat Resort be seated on a 30-acre environmentally annoying possessions in Pune, Maharashtra. The scheme pursues highpoint local characteristics and outdated understanding in the expression of mutual international terminologies of inflexible existing and goblet constructions. The Retreat distinct lives in neanearlylf the belongings, with the conveniences of the alternative itself presence, constrained to a smaller amount than 20% of the belongings extent.

The Recourse is well-versed profoundly by outdated edifice outstanding to which the constructed form was progressed as a succession of communal and isolated places cooperative actions evocative of the municipality's past. The customer is required to generate a source of revenue occasions and arouse the indigenous economical, which was reproduced finished the setting and the enterprise inhabited by picturesque countryside and a succession of man-made ponds. Considerable of the construction substantial was obtained from round the position.

Vernacular Architecture of the North

Gravels taken out from adjacent aquatic bodies are working in an assortment of vernacular methods that variety from the dehydrated carton and outfitted stonework to compound rock tangible. Substances such as stone bright furnishings were obtained from artists from adjacent settlements and charitable improvement to the native artistry.

Although the preceding Pavilions helped mostly as an addressee for performances, the 2018 Pavilion envisioned a supplementary inclusive programmatic use of interplanetary. This encompassed spaces for workshops, discourses, communal recitals, meetings and book introductions, and encompassed two cafeterias, a youngsters' art expanse and a biological excess reprocessing unit. To dwell in the unabridged position, the building was critiqued and started to complete as a landmass middle for sculpture with the individuals.

The construction removed its stimulus from the local presentation tent. Utilizing vernacular resources like timber, and cane, in addition, to other seeming surfaces in a mixture with contemporary materials like steel sections and glass, the tent explores the possibility of diffusing its opacity and heaviness although pervading it with brightness and convenience. The constructions are intended to be seated "lightly" on the position.

Vernacular Architecture of the North

The rotunda is intended to be totally dismantled into types of machinery salvageable for reuse, to permit for the site's rewarding finished the impending two years.

The double-skin frontage generates a semi-permeable coating that assistances in covering and adaptable the infection among the external and inner surroundings through a skilful airflow. It distances tallness of three grounds, possession in attention physical honesty and trembling confrontation, transported to lifetime finished a widespread framework and moulding procedure. The interior redesigned law court topographies dense plantation to decrease warmth gain through evaporative refrigeration.

Supplementary resources secondhand in the edifice of this refuge slab encompasses tangible in numerous methods and strengthen segments for the movement provision arrangements. The hostel's enterprise authorizes scholars with the autonomy of crusade inside a situation that arranges current luxury and functionality to develop a paradigm of nil liveliness project.

The draftswomen intentional the metropolis's philosophy and topography, enchanting motivation from the aboriginal structure practices like Garhwali *'kholis'* and the *'dhajji'* (divided floorings) method. The construction is concerned with the lengthways of the East-West alliance and the dominant admission rifts the capability into two portions. The senses that need a chiller set are positioned on the pulverized floor, while the meanings within elevation interior warmth advance are situated on the higher ground.

Hefty operable openings in the extraordinary capacity places that take improvement of the predominant winds for aeration deliver 80% daylight spaces, as healthy as reasonable interior infections.

An essential well-lit well eradicates strips creating a well-lit public interstellar for the workforce. The structure was intended to be a net-zero construction on liveliness, aquatic and left-over, and repurposed the current substance of the big competence. The inactive enterprise policies give a sturdy architectural appearance to the construction and create spaces that produce interdependent relations.

The factual palette of the construction likewise inducements profoundly from the instantaneous topography. The practice of indigenous constituents, systems, and employment form the character of the capability and manufacture it a truthfully vernacular development.

The strategy is resulting from the customary 9x9 network and the place was scattered with opinions that wished then energy on to develop trees. Normality is attained finished the network, and unconventionality is cast-off to disrupt the instruction. Water forms are scattered over this circle that produces the liquid circle from the structure to the pulverized and annoy the climatic panels whilst generating opinions of exchange.

Existence in Seismic Zone 2, a slender, vernacular technique of producing physical firmness has accepted consent for the formation of enormous distances that are well-optimised by the countryside of the interplanetary. A trifling palette of stone, crystal, brace and vinyl that is not unfocused by besides numerous exteriors is accepted to dexterity a building that is penetrating and bare-boned completely at the identical spell. The indigenous and local arrangements of countenance are discovered as energetic capitals to produce a construction that occupies the forthcoming.

The position arrangement is stimulated by traditional Himalayan villages, secure everywhere a Darbargadh, the outdated house of native rajas or nobles and includes a chief guesthouse block and a sequence of cabins in the interior. Distorting appearances amongst peripheral and interior, assembly's cataract unhappy the 12.5-acre conspiracy to deliver enclosed stream interpretations from diverse facts. The architectural database of the recourse contains a reaction, bistro, living room, tavern, boutique, consultation hall, border lodgings and a public library.

The resources castoff are native, excluding for reinforce substituting cedar ligneous rays due to ecological mistreatment apprehensions. Stream stones system the absorbent fortifications, the account is used in the slates and floorboards and large timber surrounds are a charity for woodworking. Archetypal Indian ornamental geometries illustrate the bottoms and the jalis complete of shaped determined frames.

Collective with the architectural, longitudinal and redesigning compassion of the scheme, which nurtures reliable influences to the setting, Taj Rishikesh makes the most of its colossal setting while having sufficient money for silent luxuries such as glowing.

Krushi Bhawan is a capability industrialized for the Management of Odisha's Subdivision of Farming & Farmers' Enablement. The 1,30,000 sq. managerial centre lodges approximately 600 people, totalling the communal appointment and knowledge spaces - enthused by the construction of Otto Konigsberg.

The Pulverized floor is a free-flowing community interplanetary that unlocks available into a Plaza, which postponement the road, in adding to the cooperative an education centre, a corridor, an audience, a collection, and exercise rooms. The roof has remained calculated to house built-up unindustrialized displays. The punctures in the portico benefit logically casual the construction. The dissimilar graphic uniqueness of Krushi Bhawan has remained resulting from local resources and dialect stories, spoken in a method that is receptive to the native temperature.

Modern descriptions of outdated Odia dexterity and customary Ikat drapery have also amused a portion of the enterprise fundamentals and masonry. The draftswomen reconstructed these decorations with blocks using three dissimilar colours of earthen obtained in the vicinity.

Further supplies rummage-sale in the construction embrace close by obtained laterite and khondalitestone. Krushi Bhawan has thus remained intended as an interstellar that simplifies cooperation amongst the government and its individuals, and opinions as a gratified existing sample honouring the essential of vernacular architecture.

If everything is to be occupied after vernacular architecture, it delivers a vigorous joining amongst beings and the atmosphere. It re-establishes us in our specific portion of the ecosphere and forces people to contemplate rapports of uncontaminated endurance building formerly the designer. These assemblies existing a climate-responsive method to lodging and are expected and reserve cognizant explanations to a local construction requirement. By spreading vernacular approaches to the contemporary project, an assembly can preferably accomplish remaining zero energy use, and be an exclusively self-reliant house.

The assistances of vernacular architecture obligate stood comprehended through the hefty part of history, lessened through the contemporary era, and are nowadays manufacture a reoccurrence amongst green construction and draftsmen. In command to advancement in the forthcoming of construction and maintainable edifice, **we obligation primarily gain information of the previous and employ these policies as a well-proportioned, logical complete to accomplish finest energy effectiveness.**

CHAPTER FIVE

E - East

Vernacular Architecture of Bengal:

Bengal is one of the most cultural parts of India. Every part of Bengal shows the influence of different kinds of culture. Bengal has not had so much availability of stone. In ancient Bengal, the use of brick and wood and Bamboo was noticed in almost every construction.

During different Emperor periods, there was a vast type of work experienced by the Bengal People. The different designs and structures of the building tell the stories of different eras of Bengal. India is the 5th-ranked holder country in terms of having heritage sites globally. Heritage sites that are examples of vernacular architecture are protected by ASI (Archeological Survey of India) as per the Indian law made in 1958.

Vernacular Architecture of Bengal: Fig. 1

The Architecture of Bengal is a fusion of traditional rural vernacular, colonial townhouses and country homes, contemporary urban designs, and old urban, religious, and urban styles. A significant Bengali architectural export is the bungalow design.

One of the first public structures created by the East India Company when Kolkata (Calcutta) became the de facto capital of British India was St. John's Church, which was once a cathedral. Warren Hastings, the Governor-General of India, laid the cornerstone on April 6, 1784.

The St. John's church, which was created by architect James Agg and was formerly known as the "Pasture Girja," is constructed from a combination of brick and stone (Stone Church). The stones were transported down the Hooghly River from the ancient remains of Gour.

The church is a sizable quadrilateral building designed in the Neoclassical style. Its most notable feature is a spire made of stone that is 176 feet tall. A massive clock that is wound daily is housed in the spire.

In the 18th century, Tagore's grandfather constructed Jorasanko Thakurbari. The two "Shankar" or Shiva temples, known as Jora Shankar, that are close to the house gave it its name. Indian Classical Fine Arts were developed at Jorasanko Thakurbari. The Rabindra Bharati Museum, which was founded in 1961, is another wonderful museum that is located there. This museum is one of the most well-liked tourist destinations for both Indian and international visitors thanks to its collection of Tagore's works.

The Natya Mancha, which is located in the middle of the house, may be viewed from the mansion's wraparound verandah by residents.

The Rasmancha is a legacy building situated at Bishnupur, Bankura locale, West Bengal, India. It was approved by Mallabhum ruler Hambir Malla Dev in 1600 CE. The length and expansiveness of this sanctuary is 26.5 meter and the level is 14.5 meter. The special stepped area of the sanctuary is made of laterite stone and the upper part is made with blocks. The upper piece of the structure seems to be a pyramid. The central part is motivated by Bengali hovels and the curves of the lower part look like Islamic designs. During the Vaishnava Ras celebration, all the Radha Krishna symbols of Bishnupur town are carried here to be revered by the residents. The General Mailing station, Kolkata, is the main mailing station of the city of Kolkata, India. The General Mailing station was worked in 1864 by Walter B. Grenville (1819-1874), who went about as a counselling draftsman to the public authority of India from 1864 to 1868.

The flight of stairs at the eastern side of the GPO features a metal plate, which denotes the eastern finish of the Old Post William. As of late, a marble plaque has been introduced on the Eastern walls of GPO, which includes the

Metal Plate.

Loved by the idea of the traditional European style of the Italian Renaissance, this great castle was planned by the well-known Koch ruler Maharaja Nripendra Narayan in 1888. Raised on a storm cellar of 1.5 meters in level, this two-celebrated block building covers an area of 4800 square meters. It stretches out 120 meters from north to south and 100 meters from east to west.

A yard is extended in the middle to give the primary access to the structure through the Durbar Lobby, which is dodecagonal in shape, laying on four curves upheld by huge Corinthian pilasters and extending a light at the top. The intrados of the vault is recessed in ventured designs and flanked by a little overhang with twelve window openings at the base.

Bengal Plain land Architecture:

Vernacular Architecture of Bengal: Fig. 2

The do-Chala, otherwise called Ek-Bangla, is a design that has two inclining rooftops with bent mouldings that meet at bent edges. As far as the inner design, there is a rectangular chamber, which is encased under a vaulted rooftop. This specific style mirrors the single-celled cottages of the State and has been adjusted even in Islamic Engineering.

The Single Chala sanctuaries have four rectangular rooftops meeting at a certain point. The edges of the Chala, alongside the mouldings, are cut. It is a seriously uncommon material style, taking everything into account, and you will just find a couple of designs with this material style in Nadia, Murshidabad, and Birbhum regions.

The At-Chala can be best depicted as a variety of the Burn Chala sanctuary. Consider a Single Chala sanctuary with a shortened rooftop and another Scorch Chala sanctuary added on top of it, and that is precisely how the top of an At-Chala sanctuary seems to be. This type of material is generally noted in Hugli, Medinipur, Howrah, and Bankura areas. The Malancha Dakshina Kali sanctuary in Medinipur is the best illustration of the At-Chala material style.

The Ratna configuration shows a noticeable deviation from the inclining or Chala material styles. The rooftop in these Centuries is level, and it is conquered by apexes, known as ratnas or churas. The beginning of this style is hazy because there are both Islamic and Hindu points of reference for designs that have one turret or more than that.

These level roofed styles of the sanctuary became well known during the nineteenth 100 years, particularly in the area of Medinipur. As a matter of fact, in Medinipur, there is a reasonable differentiation made between the enormous level rooftops, known as dalan, and the more modest level rooftop known as Chandni. The Rupesvara sanctuary in Kalna and the Raghunatha sanctuary in Bardhaman are genuine instances of Dalan material style.

Vernacular Architecture of Bengal: Fig. 3

The origin of the bungalow has its roots in the vernacular architecture of Bengal. The term baṅgalo, meaning "Bengali" and used elliptically for a "house in the Bengal style". Such houses were traditionally small, only one storey and detached, and had a wide veranda were adapted by the British, who used them as houses for colonial administrators in summer retreats in the Himalayas and compounds outside Indian cities. Bungalow-style houses are still very popular in rural Bengal. In the rural areas of Bangladesh, it is often called "Bangla Ghar" (Bengali Style House). The main construction material used in modern times is corrugated steel sheets. Previously they had been constructed from wood, bamboo, and a kind of straw called "Khar". Khar was used on the roof of the Bungalow house and kept the house cold during hot summer days. Another roofing material for Bungalow houses has been red clay tiles.

The Genesis and Bungalow have their roots in the Bengal region. The term bayhgalo, meaning "Bengali" and used for a "Bengali Style House". Such houses were traditionally very small, only one storey or detached and had a large veranda adopted by the British, who used them as homes for the colonial administration during summer vacations in the Himalayan region and groups of cities outside of India. The style of Bungalow homes is very popular in rural Bengal. In rural Bangladesh, they are often called "Bangla Ghar" (Bengal-style houses). The main building material used in modern times is crumpled steel sheets. Previously they were built with wood, bamboo and a straw called "Khar". Khari was used on the roofs of the Bungalow House and kept the house cool on the hot summer days. Another material for Bungalow's homes was red clay tiles.

History of Bengal plain land Architecture:

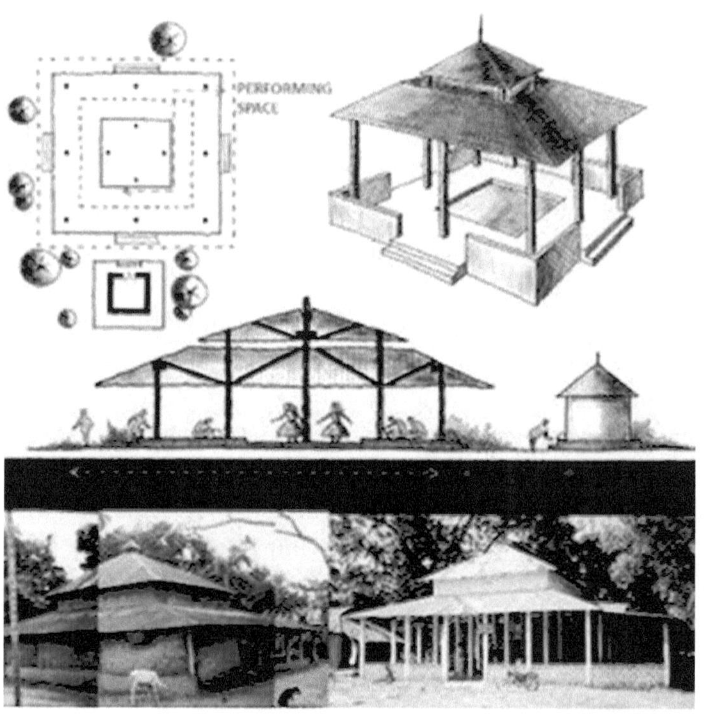

Vernacular Architecture of Bengal: Fig. 4

Due to the unavailability of stone in the plain land area of Bengal people used to start using easily available bamboo, Wood, dry grass etc material to make a shelter. The Sun dried or burnt brick made from clay was also very ductile and easy to get into the desired shape. In the medieval period, Buddhism held a stronghold in Bengal. Most of the Temples were made before the Muslim conquest was small and was built in the Gupta era and sena dynasty.

The term deula, deul or deoul is utilized for a style of Jain and Hindu sanctuary design of Bengal, where the sanctuary comes up short on common mandapa close to the fundamental sanctum, and the principal unit comprises just of the holy place and a deul above it. The sort emerged between the sixth and tenth hundreds of years, and most models are currently ruining; it was resuscitated in the sixteenth to the nineteenth century.

Most sanctuaries making due in sensible condition date from about the seventeenth century onwards, after sanctuary building restored; it had halted after the Muslim victory in the thirteenth century. The material style of Bengali Hindu sanctuary engineering is novel and firmly connected with the paddy roofed customary structure style of country Benga.

Material styles incorporate the jor-bangla, do-Chala, singe Chala, at-Chala, and Ek-Ratna. The do-Chala type has just two hanging rooftop tips on each side of a rooftop separated in the centre by an edge line; in the uncommon scorch Chala type, the two rooftop parts are combined into one unit and have a vault-like shape; the twofold story at-Chala type has eight rooftop corners.

A considerable lot of these sanctuaries are covered on the external walls with earthenware (cut block) reliefs. Bishnupur in West Bengal has a surprising arrangement of the seventeenth and eighteenth-century sanctuaries with an assortment of rooftop styles worked by the Malla line.

In bigger, and later, sanctuaries, little pinnacles ascend from the middle or corners of the bending rooftop. These are straight-sided, frequently with tapered rooftops. They have little similarity to a common north Indian shikhara sanctuary tower. The Pancha Ratna ("five pinnacles") and navaratna ("nine pinnacles") styles are assortments of this type.

The sanctuary structures contain gabled rooftops which are conversationally called the Chala, For instance, a gabled rooftop with an eight-sided pyramid organized rooftop will be designated "ath Chala" or in a real sense the eight essences of the rooftop. Furthermore, oftentimes there is more than one pinnacle in the sanctuary building. These are works of laterite and block bringing them helpless before the serious atmospheric conditions of southern Bengal. Dakshineswar Kali Sanctuary is one illustration of the Bhanja style while the extra little sanctuaries of Shiva along the waterway bank are illustrations of southern Bengal rooftop style however in a much more modest aspect.

In this mod technology-based era, it is very important to preserve vernacular architecture. These architecture are examples of the history of heritage and culture of a particular era or region. India is the 5th-ranked holder country in terms of having heritage sites globally. Heritage sites that are examples of vernacular architecture are protected by ASI(Archeological Survey of India)as per the Indian law made in 1958. This architecture may damage due to several reasons like natural damage, Air pollution, Fungus, temperature changes etc.

The research shows that Due to a lack of skilled manpower there is a serious issue to carry forward the architectural process in future. The vernacular architecture is given the least priority to preservation from damage. Also, skilled resources are unavailable for vernacular architecture.

The three main methods used for heritage conservation are structural reinforcement, repair work on walls, ceilings and removal of weeds, and awareness programs to help people understand the importance of preserving old buildings. Chemical Conservation protects the environment by preventing the release of harmful gasses. Helps eliminate moss, algae, and lichens.

It can be concluded from the above study that Bengal has various types of vernacular architecture and it is influenced by the people of a different era. It has a great influence on the history and the culture of Bengal. It can be preserved in various ways to show the history and culture of Bengal. With the help of Modern Technology, The vernacular architecture can be improved in features so that the fusion of the vernacular and modern technology can be a great example worldwide.

Vernacular Architecture in the Eastern Hills:

Eastern India a paradise unexplored. It has a rich treasure of traditions and is a delight for tourists and well, a pride for its inhabitants. North East India has its own Vernacular architecture which it has developed through ages and is an integral part of its cultural background.

Vernacular architecture is the architectural style that is designed based on the local needs, availability of construction materials and hereby reflecting local traditions.

Vernacular Architecture in the Eastern Hills: Fig. 5

Architectural typologies have evolved in North East India as a factor of traditional heritage, their climate and functionality. The north east region of India is a small sized region having one of the highest biodiversity densities in the world. Its formidable terrain consists of mountains, hills, rain-forests, river, and jungles, which remain comparatively unexplored resulting in a lack of infrastructure and growth. But, the lack of infrastructure has helped prevail the vernacular style of housing both unique and traditional to the local tribes.

Arunachal and their settlement pattern

The houses of tribes of Arunachal Pradesh represent their dwellings and their size depends on the family pattern of the tribe.

Architecture in Arunachal. Fig. 6

The typical house consists of sora ghar, Huwa ghar and Randhani ghar. The sora ghar or drawing room is a public place for gathering or meeting relatives or visitors. This room houses the 'Dhenki' or pounding machine it has a common fireplace called 'Jui Hali' over which hanging platforms are kept for storing household items. The Huwa ghar or the bedroom is a partitioned space depending on number of married sons and number of family members. The last room is Randhoni ghar or kitchen space that serves as dining room for the family.

The Adi gallong folk of Sian district

Adi means Hill man or man of hills, they are a large tribe, inhabiting the unspoiled valleys of Brahmaputra River during its course in South Tibet. They are noteworthy for their bridges, cane suspension bridges and are quiet a showcase of native ingenuity.

The size of the houses depends on the size of the family. The traditional houses are built with bamboos, woods, canes and leaves. Their houses are raised well above the ground with the help of stilts and on these stilts, wooden beams are tied to make a level flooring. Their roofs are made by dry paddy straws, dry Tokow leaves or thatched grass. No nails were used in their construction and the houses had two doors. One in front for the men and the other at the back for women.

Vernacular Architecture of Nagaland

Nagaland is one of the most colorful states of India. Its settlement pattern is largely a result of custom of head hunting, formerly prevalent through the Naga cultural realm. Climate plays an important factor in influencing its settlement pattern.

Enter Caption

Sema Tribe

Sema villages exist in the hilly parts of Nagaland. They are usually built in the summit of a hill or on shoulder of a spur. Where the climate is hot like near the valley of river Dayang, a summit is usually chosen but in colder regions a shoulder below the ridge of a range of hills is a common site for a village. All the houses within the same village are of same style for one to be immediately able to identify which tribe a particular village belongs to. Semas were head hunters, their captured enemy would be beheaded and their heads hung up.

Their primary construction materials included Timber, or structural elements like posts, Bamboo for walls and other structural elements and Thatch for roofing material.

Kutcha Houses:

The houses made from organic renewable materials such as bamboo, mud, grass, straw and leaves are Kutcha houses. The plinth and the foundation consist of consolidated earth with timber or bamboo posts. The walls would consist of bamboo mats and split bamboo framings, grass, cane leaves and so on. The 'Kutcha houses' in North East India also have different forms, due to micro climatic differences and cultural beliefs.

Vernacular Architecture in the Eastern Hills: Fig. 2

Vernacular Architecture of Arunachal Pradesh

The houses of tribes of Arunachal Pradesh represent their dwellings and their size depends on the family pattern of the tribe.

The typical house consists of sora ghar, Huwa ghar and Randhani ghar. The sora ghar or drawing room is a public place for gathering or meeting relatives or visitors. This room houses the 'Dhenki' or pounding machine it has a common fireplace called 'Jui Hali' over which hanging platforms are kept for storing household items. The Huwa ghar or the bedroom is a partitioned space depending on number of married sons and number of family members.

The last room is Randhoni ghar or kitchen space that serves as dining room for the family.

The Adi tribe

Adi means Hill man or man of hills, they are a large tribe, inhabiting the unspoiled valleys of Brahmaputra River during its course in South Tibet. They are noteworthy for their bridges, cane suspension bridges and are quiet a showcase of native ingenuity.

The size of the houses depends on the size of the family. The traditional houses are built with bamboos, woods, canes and leaves. Their houses are raised well above the ground with the help of stilts and on these stilts, wooden beams are tied to make a level flooring. Their roofs are made by dry paddy straws, dry Tokow leaves or thatched grass. No nails were used in their construction and the houses had two doors. One in front for the men and the other at the back for women.

The Nyishi tribe

It is the single largest tribe of the state. They are experts in handicrafts and maintain a high degree of self-sufficiency. Their houses are constructed with wood and bamboo, using thatch, Chinese palm leaves, Cane leaves and Jungle banana leaves as roofing material based on availability. The floors of houses are raised 2.5 meters from the ground and ceiling, 2.5 meters from the floor level. The plan consists of Verandah, common room with fire place, bed room, guest room, front verandah and side verandah. Their kitchen cum fire place, 'emmi', its base is constructed with bamboo support on the surface of the room, foot wooden blocks on banana leaves and then soil is applied upon the height of the blocks, thus the stove can be laid for kitchen purpose.

Both Adi and Nyshi tribe structure of housing is very earthquake resistant as bamboo and wood are very light and hence the damage to the life and property is henceforth minimized.

Vernacular Architecture of Nagaland

Nagaland is one of the most colorful states of India. Its settlement pattern is largely a result of custom of head hunting, formerly prevalent through the Naga cultural realm. Climate plays an important factor in influencing its settlement pattern.

Sema Tribe

Sema villages exist in the hilly parts of Nagaland. They are usually built in the summit of a hill or on shoulder of a spur. Where the climate is hot like near the valley of river Dayang, a summit is usually chosen but in colder regions a shoulder below the ridge of a range of hills is a common site for a village. All the houses within the same village are of same style for one to be immediately able to identify which tribe a particular village belongs to. Semas were head hunters, their captured enemy would be beheaded and their heads hung up.

Their primary construction materials included Timber, or structural elements like posts, Bamboo for walls and other structural elements and Thatch for roofing material.

Enter Caption

Vernacular Architecture of Meghalaya

Garo Tribe

Garo traditional tribal architecture is a magnificent example of vernacular architecture. They build functional structures from bamboo mainly for living and storage, but they also do it beautifully. The houses are built on stilts and lower aces are sued for storage and poultry. The roofs are sloped for extreme rainfall in this region.

Garo village hosts a dance festival where girls dance around boys who they wish to marry. All houses are ordered around a courtyard where the dance is performed, adjoining is a communal house and the young boy's dormitory protected by a flowery enclosure. The occupation of people in this place is mainly poultry and management.

Vernacular Architecture of Manipur

Meitis are re the dominant tribe in Manipur, but the state is also home to Nagas, Kukis and Rongmis. A common house is made of bamboo, cane, wood and thatch. It may have a verandah as a gathering place, sleeping quarters, a kitchen fireplace and outhouses for livestock. The houses are usually rectangular in shape with the front part of the house comprising living room being larger than other sections. Wooden planks are used as beds the sleeping rooms which incorporates their vastu. The bed in the bedroom is usually on the northern side, the fireplace on south eastern side. The kitchen however has a fireplace right in the center, where it has racks to hang meat and fish.

Meitei Yumjao

They have complete straw reinforced mud thick wall up to the roof height embedding the main load post bearing bamboos with 'Pungjei' in different heights as reinforcement steel rods. They had specific separate spaces for separate functions reflecting their respect, privacy, and identity given to each member of the family.

Vernacular Architecture of Mizoram

Zawlbuk house

They use wood and bamboo to build tribal houses on sloping lands. Houses have wooden supports and bamboo matting is affixed to the frames and the floor. Some houses are built on slits with a small ladder for access. Houses are rectangular and the interior is partitioned into rooms using bamboo screens or mats. A raised fire place is at one corner next to the front door.

The flooring of the house is done using split bamboo and the finishing is done using flattened bamboo even the columns are made out of bamboo. Bamboo is flattened to make tremendous design patterns. The roof is made of bamboo purloins or GI sheets and rafters which are then covered with thatch.

Vernacular Architecture of Tripura

Tripura is a landlocked state in North East India. The general houses are rectangular in shape and are similar too bamboo kutcha houses with linear planning and rooms opening into each other. The structure above is formed by horizontal members tied across the bamboo posts with jute ropes using a dowel and tenon joints. The stilt height is around 1.5 to 2 meters above the ground and the space below is used to store a canoe for emergency during floods. They are typically designed to keep out the effect of heavy monsoon. The floor and the wall inlays are mostly bamboo weaves which allows the water of floods and heavy rains to pass through rather than getting stored. The roof is made by fixing bamboo trusses over the posts over which local grass is laid. A bamboo loft is fixed below the roof inside for secure storage of goods in case of floods. Bamboo, being a bad conductor of heat keeps the interiors cool and adequate ventilation through the permeable floors and wall keeps the moisture content inside the houses low

The Riang house

Riang tribals of Tripura built their houses with bamboo as the primary material for construction. In some cases, even thatched roof is made of bamboo leaves. They are typical hill dwelling constructed on bamboo slits to create large horizontal platform, the floor of the house. The posts are arranged in a square grid and inclined whole bamboo members strengthen these. The plan of the houses is rectangular with a covered verandah at the front and an open one at the back, a large enclosed room between the verandahs.

Vernacular Architecture of Assam

The state of Assam is well known for wildlife, archeological sites and tea plantations. The vernacular style of Assam mainly consists of three important significances Hip(or Gable) Roof, use of bamboo as major building material land higher plinth level.

The walls are of timber frame work, inside those panels 'ikra' is used to fill. The ikras are cut in size of panel and laid vertically. After application of ikra, it is left for two days and then plastered in both side with mud mortar. Three layers of plaster are done alternatively after during of each coat. The finished coat is a mixture of mud and cow dung. The buildings are of maximum two stories and are symmetrical on both sides. A typical Assam house has timber posts either embedded or bolted into RCC base and the house is framed with either timber and bamboo.

Chang House

Other type of traditional houses of Assam includes Chang houses. These houses are age old structures originating in the Himalayan region. In North East India the houses on slits are mainly amongst thick vegetation, forest and by the banks of the river. Traditionally, people of Mishing community of Assam used to live in these kinds of houses. They have a big hall and a central kitchen for a large joint family.

Mud Houses

These houses are made out of mud, being a mixture of soil, silt and clay to some proportion. The typical plan dimensions include lengths 5-10 meters and width 3 to 5 meters. The building has 1-2 stories. It's typical span of roofing/ flooring system is 3-4 meters. Typically, the ratio of length to breadth of the house is 3:2 or 2:1.

It is very well said that bamboo that bends is stronger than oak that resists. Though this phrase is often used metaphorically, it holds a very significant essence. Bamboo as we realise is grown and cultivated widely in north eastern regions of India. Bamboo is an extremely versatile material, its possibilities in world of making are literally endless. It is an extremely quality load- distributing structural element to be explore the walls and floors. In North eastern parts of India, versatility is sizably ignored. Deep rooted in their culture this material holds a great significance n the livelihood in terms of food, fodder and business. It is a combination of social and cultural parts of their lives. Amidst the hearts of eastern states of India, re houses of bamboo, so rich in heritage, technology and practicality. These houses are built in these ways to avoid earthquakes and monsoon.

The research makes us conclude that the architecture of North East India relates to socio-economic setup, the cultural identities and a good climatic responsiveness. A great deal of climatic response design features is revealed including temperature control, natural ventilation, protection from natural calamities such as floods, earthquakes etc. However certain features still lack in the traditional housing, like fire proneness and termite infestation due to usage of non-treated bamboo and wood, the lack of damp proofing and the use of non-stabilized soil for construction to pose problems like dampness of walls and washouts during rainfall.

CHAPTER SIX

W – West

Vernacular Architecture of Rajasthan

Rajasthan, India's largest state is indeed the most colorful state in India. The tales of its unique architecture has been heard by us all. The architecture of Rajasthan is mainly based on Rajput school of architecture, which is a unique blend of Hindu and Muslim structural designs. It's intricately carved temples, the stupendous forts and the grand havelis are an integral part of the architectural heritage of the state.

The term 'vernacular' means native and here vernacular architecture depicts native science of building. The architecture of this kind is not built by professional architects but by unschooled local builders from locally available materials, reflecting local traditions.

A Haveli in Rajasthan

Bhunga houses

These are traditional houses are designed to minimize the damage of earthquakes. They consist of a unique round mud hut with circular walled and thatched roof. These beautiful houses are built using mud and well, locally available materials like clay, timber, bamboo and so on. Such houses are termed as 'Architecture without architect' as they are not built by any highly schooled architects but by locals with their years of knowledge gained through years. The design of houses is such that it keeps the interiors cool during summer where as warm during winters and well, are tremendously strong to withstand any kinds of natural calamities like earthquakes.

A Bhunga house

It has cylindrical shaped rooms with conical roofs which is placed on two thick wooden posts, and these bear the weight of the roof. Lower levelled wooden framed widows are present for cross ventilation. The low hanging roofs extending beyond the walls protect it from direct sunlight and harsh dessert winds, while maintain a comfortable temperature on the insides.

The thatched roof present on the top of walls is built using bamboo sticks to form a cone. These sticks are tied together using dried grass rope and a very thick layer of grass is simply kept on the top. Even the walls are held together using dried grass rope and cow dung or mud is used as plaster. These houses require regular maintenance with application of lime plastering to the walls and also regular replacement of dried grass. a

Marwari and Shekhawati Havelis

The Marwaris built Havelis in Shekhawati and Marwar in around 1900s. They had huge gates and magnificent paintings on all sides. The architectural design of Havelis evolved in response to climate, lifestyle and material availability. Inner porches in buildings were thought to be the most ideal in hot weather. It served well for both hot climate and for light to enter. The courtyards were made, based on vastu shastra, depicting all areas radiate from a single point which is the core of the house. Yards are extremely prevalent in South Asian Architecture. The Chowk or the yard has separate spaces for men and women for their privacy. The local traditions and customs have an impact on the decorative features of the Havelis.

Shekhawati Haveli

Featured elements of the Havelis include-

Chhatri

These are dome shaped elevated pavilions of Indo-Islamic Architecture and one of the finest examples of Rajasthani Architecture. The word 'Chhatri' signifies tent or umbrella, it is a mark of pride and honor. It is supported by four pillars.

Jaali/jali

The ornate latticework of windows is called 'jali'. Purdah conscious made the women of the house enjoy the view of the outside world through these jalis without been seen. The exquisite play of light and the shadow is an extremely essential feature of Rajasthan's Havelis and palaces. They reflect the sun's rays and provide a cool breeze.

Jharokha

It is a type of overhanging enfolded balcony built of stones which is commonly seen in temples, Havelis and palaces in Rajasthan. They are widely used to enhance architectural elegance to palaces. The overhanging balcony is an essential component in Rajasthani architecture serving both as ornamentation tool and observation desk.

Stepwells

They are also called as Bawdis. It is well or a pond that can be reached by a stepping down a flight of stairs. They are historically dug very deep into the trenches of the Earth to obtain consistent groundwater throughout the year. The trench barriers were constructed of stone blocks without the use of any mortar and additional steps leading to the lake body were created.

Some cities of Rajasthan and their architecture

Jaipur

Jaipur is the capital and the largest city of the state of Rajasthan. It is also known as pink city and Paris of India, because of its original construction with pink sandstones. The construction of this city started around 1727 and it took around four years to complete the roads, palaces and the square. The city was built according to the Shilpa Shastra, the science of Indian Architecture.

A Haveli in Jaipur

The direction of each street and markets are east to west and north to south. The Eastern gate is called the Suraj(sun) pol while western gate is called Chand(moon) pol. The city was originally within walls, it expanded outside of original walls with time. The town of Jaipur is built in the form of eight-part mandala known as 'Pithapada'. The basic features include a courtyard to support ventilation, big windows with low sill and high ceilings to increase comfort levels. Stone is the basic construction unit where lime is used as binding material. Big stone pillars are used in elevations, there is complete rubble masonry and Kota stone flooring.

The zoning in high profile house included the right half as the public zone or men's area while the left half being the private zone, bedrooms for the ladies, kitchen and dining. Bedrooms were in southwest while pooja and study houses were in the north. As the buildings were built in the colonial period it reflects the elements of influence like pillars and arches. Its façade is colored white blended with Jaipur style.

The Havelis of Jaipur are multistoried buildings with rooms facing an inner courtyard they are generally built of red sandstone or brick with lime mortar. The Haveli principle was developed to contend with extreme climate and to satisfy socio cultural requirements. Courtyards were kept to keep the interior private. Where possible women kept their privacy in zenana. High walls with pierced screens for air and limited views helped maintain privacy along with careful use of bamboo blinds(chiks) and curtains (pardas). Most of the rooms in havelis were flexible with soft furnishing it had grand receptions for receiving formal visitors or family functions. Smaller reception rooms were required for business offices and raised platforms (chabutras) served as inevitable waiting rooms.

Udaipur

Present in the bow shaped basin of Aravalli ranges in southern Rajasthan, Udaipur is also called the city of lakes. It is compared to European city, Venice for its romantic appeal. The heritage fabric of the city creates harmony between its natural elements and built form. The ancient city is sacred place with respect to administration, architecture and heritage. The most dominating feature of Udaipur is Lake Pichola which is the urban fabric representing development of historic core. This lake influences favorable changes in micro climate of region where people are faced with low humidity, scorching heat and glare. The built form uses cooling quality of water increases visual scale and well, the prominence of palaces built around it.

The town is often associated with the presence of marvelous lake palace which reflects the wealth and valor of Mewar kingdom. The city palace embodies the history of Sisodia royal dynasty. The city palace is separated by several chowks, courtyards and having gardens. Jagdish Chowk is the center layout of the city due presence of Jagdish temple.

The most prevalent feature of buildings here is 'cusped' or 'peacock' arch supported by fluted columns which is a highlight of Rajput architecture. Their windows have tinted glass and are often used with screens to reduce solar radiation and offer privacy. The remarkable features of Rajput architecture include the presence of expansive balconies creating a visual link with the water bodies, the use of sandstones, whitewashed walls of havelis with marvelous 'chattrison' towers and forts and arched elements over doorways and windows.

The havelis consisted of three courtyards. One outside the haveli for evening walks, tying of domestic animals and to celebrate special occasions. A central courtyard for family gets togethers, morning prayers, holding feast and children playing. The last one with zenana for crushing spices, drying masalas, grinding wheat and get together of women.

Jaisalmer

The city is located in the midst of great Indian Desert on the western frontier of India. It is almost entirely a sandy waste forming a part of Thar dessert. In west they are covered with long bushes and in east with tufts of long grass.

People in Jaisalmer lived in forts, now many of them have been converted to shops. They used golden stone for construction. They didn't use any mortar but made bonds using scissors in-between the golden stones. Since golden stones are soft stones, carvings are easier on it.

Dust storms were prevalent in this area and hence all major streets were oriented in east- west direction at right angles to the direction of the sand storms. The interiors of buildings were protected by almost blank walls with very small openings.

Hindu Merchants and their Havelis

The Havelis of the Hindu merchants in Rajasthan were very similar to other Havelis of Rajasthan, just adapted to the beliefs and customs of the Hindu merchants. The Havelis were internally divided into two distinct portions, a 'mardankhana' (male quarters) and a shielded 'zanankhana' (female quarters), each having its own courtyard. These havelis always had a direct entrance into the front or male section and an indirect entrance with a baffle wall into the female section. The special feature of Hindu traders Havelis was the presence of a kitchen or 'rasoda' with 'chulha'(hearth) on one side of the court.

Brahmin Caste and Their Havelis

The Havelis of the Brahmins were very similar to the Hindu Merchants. They also had two distinct portions in their Havelis separate for men and women. The special aspect in these Havelis was the presence of Kitchen on the top floors and it is for the same reason for which the Brahmin Havelis of Bhatt and Kasliwal in Jaipur, had 'parinda' formed as a small enclosure near the staircase landing. 'Parinda' was a space for keeping water which was usually a small room on one side of the inner court, but accustomed to the Brahmin architecture in Rajasthan.

Rajputs and Their Havelis

Symbol of luxury and, power and strength, Rajputana structures define an era of architecture brilliance. The morphology of the Rajasthan exhibits the use of different design elements like courtyard, jaali, jharokha, water bodies, etc. From the above-mentioned elements various elements amongst them perform multiple functions, for example-water bodies helps in thermal cooling and also act as aesthetic feature and a gathering place. Courtyard acts as a source of ventilation and also built a relation between indoor and outdoor. Jaali serves us with many functions like ventilation, privacy and aesthetics. All the above-mentioned design elements have been used in the buildings of the Rajasthan for heating and ventilation.

Hawa Mahal

Hawa Mahal is additionally called the palace of winds. It has 953 small jharokha or covered windows. This 16th century carved jali catches the breeze using principles found in modern air conditioning, offering both security and air circulation. It works on the principle of venturi effect and Bernoulli theorem. Venturi principle states that air is compressed and increases its speed when passed through a funnel causing a breeze.

Construction Techniques and Materials of The Region

All the communities have their own building style and architecture depending on the local availability and is evolved to meet the challenges of a unique set of conditions. Both timber and timber and hard pans are a major building resource. Materials include mud, adobe or sun-dried bricks, lime and lime mortar. Almost all buildings in Rajasthan are constructed using different types of sandstones depending upon local availability. Sand stone is good insulator and poor conductor. It reflects most of the sun light and allows very little heat to pass through. In these havelis a system of modular construction is used, in which cutting the sandstone into standardized columns, beams and floor slabs could be arranged in endless permutations and combinations to give the havelis a unique character and kinship with its neighbors.

Vernacular Architecture of Gujarat

Lying on the western coast of India, Gujarat is home to diverse beliefs and ethnicities. Varied varieties of houses are present in Gujrat from bamboo houses in south Gujrat to circular earth construction houses at Kutch.

Vernacular architecture is also known as architecture without architects and architecture of this kind is the most economical architecture.

The best instance of dwelling typology can be seen in bhunga houses at Banni, Kutch. These huts are constructed by craftspeople people and constitute mud walls and thatch roofs. Though they lack visual charm from the idea, they have elaborate mud and mirror work with coupled murals and frescos on the interiors.

There are three main varieties of urban houses in Gujrat namely North Gujrat, South Gujrat and Saurashtra.

Vadodara, a city in Gujrat.

Rathva Tribe

Rathva Tribe is an Adivasi community living in the state of Gujrat. Their landscape used to comprise 20-25 houses belonging to a few lineages scattered on hill tops and gradual slopes of over 5 kilometers. Their houses were set apart from each other by Jawar and Maize fields. Their houses were made facing the east, rectangular in structure. The roof was made of split bamboo covered with baked clay tiles or dried palm leaves. The walls were made of split bamboo plastered with mixture of cow dung, straw and mud. The Rathvas had a parallel structure built close to their houses with no partition walls, for cattle and goats.

Rathva House

Sociology and planning of North Gujrat

A few provinces in India where the architectural traditions are so well preserved as even till date in Gujrat. The ancient culture of Gujrati culture was north Gujrat, roughly the areas between Narmada in the South and hills of Danta in the north. The urban lifestyle which evolved in north Gujrat became a dominant model for the rest of the province and resulted in a remarkably homogeneous and uniform urban pattern over a widespread area. The culture which arose in the medieval parts of Gujrat was inspired by active and dominant mercantile community and not feudal elements as the rest of India. Evidence of which can be seen even today in the demographic structure of the town. In every major town the central prized locations are occupied by financers, traders, manufacturers and artisans.

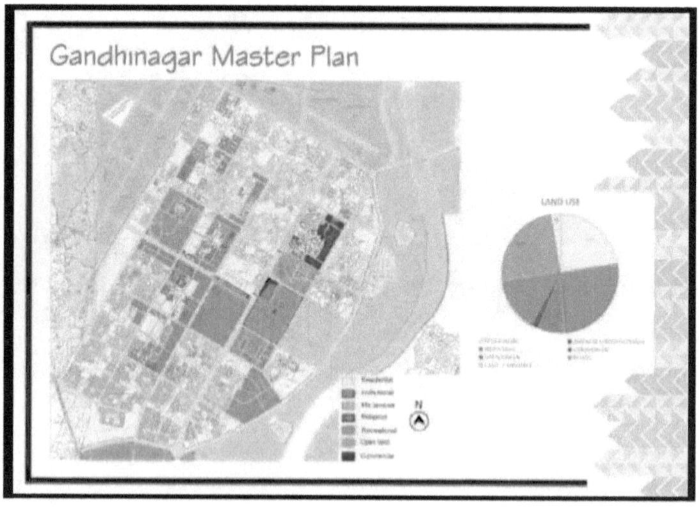

Masterplan of South Gujarat

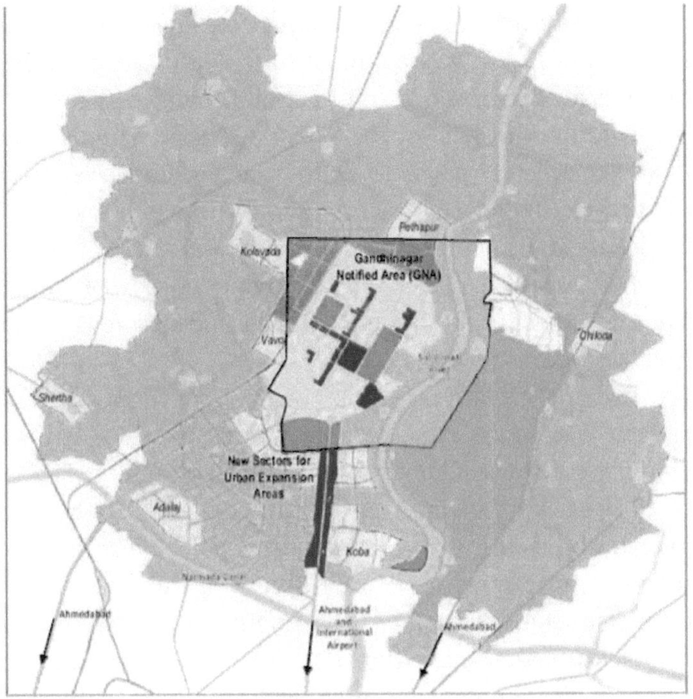

Gandhinagar Development Plan

Vernacular architecture at Kutch, Gujrat

Kutch is a district of Gujarat in western India. People in this area of the low-income category and it is an earthquake-protease-prone areas. Kutch is divided mainly into two parts, Rann of Kutch- the wet and dry region without any settlements. It has salt flat lands in summer and the hooded in the rainy season.

Kutcha houses

The plinth and the foundation of these consist of consolidated earth with stones and bamboo posts, the walls consist of mud walls, and split grass, and our roof is thatched and made of wheat and maize straws. The kutcha houses in Kutch have a common form due to the presence of micro differences and cultural Bong. Bonga is construction the type in the Kutch district of Gujrat state that is completely prone to earthquakes. A Bongo consists of a single cylindrically shaped room it also consists of conical roofs supported by cylindrical walls. This type of construction has existed for several hundreds of years. These kinds of houses are very durable and are prevalent in desert concerns.

"Kutchua" is anything the north-western portion of Gujarat is called as. Through a rich gem of custom, it is an enjoyment for travellers and arrogance for the population. North-western Gujarat has its dialect building which is industrialised through the eternities and must remain themselves within the vicinity accessible substantial, the out-dated construction is time confirmed, bearable and complex to the microclimatic situations and ordinary misfortunes, counting shakings which the north-western county is susceptible to Numerous truth-seekers and notable draftswomen like Hassan Fatty have encouraged the primary perceptions of outmoded construction to form present-day enterprise. Nevertheless improbable in the north-western province, the old-style construction has remained substituted by reckless mounting tangible rainforests, which are not maintainable or delicate in the direction of the normal disasters and microclimatic circumstances.

Bhonga Houses

The native Administration of these conditions requires to be subtle in recruiting the native regulations and preparation recommendations which endorse or permit inducement for the practice of outmoded architectural procedures and perceptions so that this problem can be undertaken accurately. The initial step in the direction of this expedition ought to be an education on the covering typologies of north-western Gujarat and the straightforward fundamental project main so that they can be successfully interpreted into contemporary projects.

The Kutch area container is alienated into three shares consecutively additional or fewer horizontally in an east-west course. The major of the three is the Rann in the northern spreading on the way to the southeast. Of this, the superior northern segment is recognised as the Rann of Kutch and the southeastern portion is recognised as Little Rann.

The household is an oblong construction fronting in the direction of the east. The rooftop is prepared of split cane enclosed with parched earthen slates or desiccated palm vegetation. The fortifications are complete of divided bamboo coated with a combination of cow manure, grass and sludge. The chief partition of the verandah transmits a blessed canvas of plethor and the adjacent wall are slight deity.

Not together since its single and amusing social inheritance, it is the existence of anthropological existences in the life-threatening climatic environments that collusions any professor of construction and clearing scholarships It has a scorching and gasping environment and one of the warmest spaces in Gujarat which is uninterruptedly populated by human beings.

The summertime is tremendously hot and the infection surpasses additional than 49°C, affectation tests for the existence of persons or for that substance slightly life procedures. Though, the darks in Kutch are attractive and calm, with the nightly fever dwindling significantly. Seasonal triumph for not quite eight months in a year. As a consequence firmament is strong in the greatest of the months with 345 sunshine days apiece year. When wintertime originates, January is the unkindest month of the day and the infection chronicled 2°C. It incomes in wintertime, existences are gleaming and the hours of darkness are actual abundant and emotionless.

As an alternative, a combination of dry parklands with lime farmhouses and infrequently coconut plantations will brand bright that Kutch has a miscellaneous scenery. Building pamphlets constructed procedure and three-dimensional governments and examines local native building- its development, construction, community and secluded seats, the procedure and seats of the characteristic households to the entire community spreading to the rudimentary procedure of urban and in conclusion the urban of Kutch.

The dominant girdle is banned prairie, a baked plain with prickly trees-ganda – a semi-recompense elongating east to west as stumpy rock-strewn hills distributed by the riverbeds and torrents, which are recurrently parched. The southern seaside part wherever aquatic convenience is upright and has practically all kinds of vegetation and wildlife with khajur and neem trees frightened in great statistics.

Habitat in a steamy climatic section is an arrangement of uncluttered, semi uncluttered and surrounded chairs interlaced collected founding the community and isolated monarchy- together named „constructed procedure" or „built atmosphere". The principles, faith, temperature, ingredients, community buildings, and reduced of the individuals of that dwelling outline the existing decoration and the environment. Equally the environment and routine reproduce the performance, community customary up, reduced as similarly the innate civilizations and the objectives of the individuals. It similarly has abundant communal constructions, communities, fortresses, shrines, mosques, honouring chattris and period boreholes, manufactured in shingle demonstrating the technique's ability to be as beautiful as timber determination.

The imprinted stonework gadkhi lamp which is niche close to the entrance and opening cranium, entrance and opening beams are decoratively decorated charitable a robust consistent character to the house facades and the street wall – forming a seamless streetscape. In the Kutch area, two distinct architectural typologies (type of buildings) are changed outstanding to dissimilar climatic, communal and economic circumstances inside the faith. The middle, cowboy movie and southern seaside part with scorching and damp weather has extended row kind households with thin roads system and impenetrable populace. These are outdated communities and people are complicated in interchange, craft and farming.

The additional payments in north reward of banni part with warm and thirsty temperature and approximately portions in the southern seaside recompense are be located in by the travelling and semi travelling countrified group of people in a humanitarian environment of impressively good-looking round mud and roofing dynasties. It has progressed by the common environments and the insufficiency of construction constituents in the punishment area.

All dynasties of the community are noise communities on in cooperation verges of the way. Many landscapes like arrivals and openings, insignia, touches and models on beams differentiate a specific household and collection. Noise covering design decreases the contact of outside partition exteriors to the sun as the portion of the household is a shared partition. The undertaking of sincere air everywhere the household is diminished and assistances to preserve the centres calm and contented. The highway breadth additional energies on slightly lessening and at their connexion are the district seats. Slender thoroughfares and tracks endure dismissing in development of interplanetary about 5-6 households which are warm communal door facades or Mangan's.

Architectural Typological industrialisation in Kutch County as Feature of Practise, Temperature and Functionality. The ingredients second-hand are nearby existing ingredients like Sludge, Cane, bamboo shrubberies, late-night Bones, pebbles etc. Bhungas are outmoded dynasties exclusive to the Kutch district in Gujarat.

The households are round and enclosed with a thatched roof. Rendering to the restraint of physical and building methods. These households are fundamentally complete from carbon-based renewable capitals such as muck, sward, intimidate manure bamboo etc. The pedestal and the substance contain combined soil with pebble and cane poles, the ramparts contain mire partition, fragmented sward, ground, bamboo etc., and the rooftop is thatched, complete of wheat or maize hays. The Mechanical Scheme contains mire load manner partition and the timber mad bind which provisions the rooftop.

The timber pillars are in the household in the mire partition. Abundant the behaviours of the construction are subject to the consignment comportment sludge bulwarks. The construction Honesty is reliant on upon colossal partition of mud. The angle Connexion is forested Twigs and the Substance are just occupied with soil with the complexity of 2-3feet. The timber in the household is nearby obtainable after the close. The foremost Construction disappointment in the area is owing to response and corrosion of ramparts owing to salinity. The Salinity corrodes the lowest share of the partition in the external lateral, so the irritating unit reductions owing to corrosion so the entire arrangement is dragged in the conflicting. So this response due to salinity grounds the construction to misrepresent and finally nose dive.

The towns of Gujarat have households which are strongly crowded and retort with all to the temperature in the scorching dry weather. These households have shared ramparts (similar row houses); they are commonly crushed positive two/three constructions move toward slender streets. This guarantees shade and coldness on the ways as well as the smallest exposure to the blistering and parched weather. The courtyard is a climatic scheme that becomes graceful and airing as the structure depth becomes too bottomless.

Given to resources used in architectural procedures, Pucca communities can be additional confidential as adapted kutcha family. Altered kutcha communities stand nearby semblance with the outdated kutcha families and are regularly actuality manufactured in the rustic extents of these existences. They are changed for the custom of current ingredients in structure. The outmoded straw gable is traded by ligneous under structure with Mangalore thatches protection in that way plummeting the upkeep of the rooftop throughout raining existences. The structure method is comparable with steadied trodden stone slabs with strengthening bars as perpendicular strengthening and straight armour-plated tangible groups at numerous heights as seismic security actions.

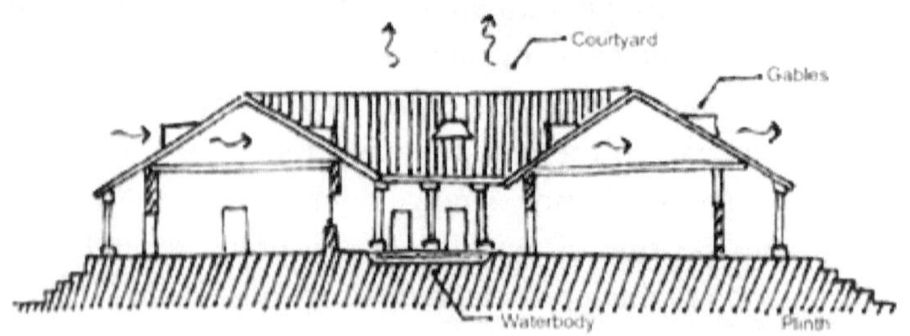

Traditional inner courtyard with a water body

In a Pol, numerous dissimilar societies may be characterized, each breathing inside its personal Khadki. Inside each Khadki there are not at all any barricades amongst individual residences, in detail, the relatives are all consistent, and the communal link between families is precise and sturdy.

Altogether communal happenings are accomplished in the mutual yard and this collective space helps to warmly connect up all the relations. This benevolent clearance decoration is distinctive for North Gujarat and people of South Gujarat anywhere wanderers on or after the north have formed individuals in groups. This is called the Khadki or North Gujarat pattern.

On the first flooring of the home, predominantly the forward-facing room has stood established to traditional dwelling for the commerce as a significance of Urbanization and commercialization. In place of it opens on view to look of each bystander was not appropriate for definite varieties of business alike jewels, luxurious fabrics and extensive trade where discussions need additional privacy.

The staircases were re-arranged consequently that they remained straight available from the tool through a gate. The khaki area was converted into an appearance foyer and was secondhand for assorted stowing. Further, the first-floor apartment was altered into bigger corporate locations which were equipped in a comfortable method.

CHAPTER SEVEN

S – South

Vernacular Architecture of South India

Vernacular architecture takes into account the needs of the people and the availability of the materials. Just like every field of architecture, it is revolutionized with time and need. Vernacular architecture is the best form of architecture as it is most cost-effective and uses locally available materials according to the basic needs. Vernacular architecture gives the simplest solutions for sustainable issues.

South India, is also called as peninsular India, consists of southern parts of India encompassing the Indian states of Andhra Pradesh, Karnataka, Kerala, Tamil Nadu, Telangana and also union territories of Puducherry and Lakshadweep.

Reginal topography

The regional topography comprises of diverse topological and climatic patterns. It is peninsular in shape like a vast inverted triangle. It is bounded on its west by the Arabian Sea and on the north by Vindhya and Satpura range.

Local climate

The maximum temperature often exceeds 40 degrees. In general, the temperature is higher on the east coast by a few degrees as compared to the west coast.

Kachacha Houses

These houses are made of bamboo, mud, thatch, and wood and therefore is a temporary structure. They need to be regularly maintained. Some forms of Kachcha houses include the following.

Kaccha House.

Variation in settlement pattern and architecture in different parts of the region

Vernacular Architecture of Kerala

Kerala is situated between the Arabian Sea to the west and western ghats to the east, it is hence blessed with abundant water. This state is roughly divided into three distinct climatic regions, they include the eastern highlands with rugged and cool mountain terrain, the central midlands the rolling hills and the western lowlands the coastal plains. Located at the extreme southern tip of the Indian subcontinent, Kerala lies near a tectonic plate and is subjected to seismic activity.

"The architecture of Kerala is influenced by Dravidian and Indian Vedic architecture."

Timber is the prime structural building material, being abundantly available in Kerala in many varieties from bamboo to teak and rosewood. The skillful choice of Timber, its artful assembly and delicate carvings for walls, roofs, and columns are a characteristic feature of Keralan architecture. Clay was used in many forms for walling, for filling timber floors and making bricks and tiles after firing in kilns. Palm leaves were used extensively for thatching the roof and making partitioned walls.

The Architecture of Kerala.

The usage of granite is mainly limited to some hilly zones. They have a skill in quarrying, and hence dressing and sculpture stones are scarce in Kerala. Soft laterite available at shallow depth can be cut easily and molded and used as building blocks. It is a local stone that gets stronger than exposed into the atmosphere. The strength of lime mortars could be increased by admixtures of vegetable juices, such enriched mortars were used for plastering and low relief work.

The common flooring included beaten earth polished with cow dung at regular intervals. Black colored traditional flooring was done in expensive buildings by missing lime, sand, coconut shell, white of egg, jaggery, coconut water and vegetable extracts. Smoothness was achieved by polishing the floor with a particular type of banana. Stone flooring, wooden flooring, burnt clay brick flooring are also some natural forms of flooring extensively used in Kerala.

The ridged roofs were pitched at angles between 30 degrees and 40 degrees. The roof is of intricately carved gables protruding from the roof, with overhangs supported by wooden brackets. It is prefabricated, different members are fixed on the ground and assembled at the top. No nails are used, but the roof is kept in position by interlocking in hole by rafters. The walls are made of timber or earth and the roof of coconut leaves. Structurally, the roof was supported by pillars on walls erected on a plinth raised from the ground for protection against dampness and insects in the tropical climate.

A Vernacular House.

Vernacular Architecture of Karnataka

Karnataka is in the southwest of India along the Arabian Sea coastlines.

The Khumb-Wooden pillars is a traditional Bunt house called Guthu Mane. Guthu manes are the traditional of Bunt community of Karnataka. It is a square complex with ample amount of space for storage all around, the pillars are made of wood. There are four doors, one on each side of the square, and the roof is of Mangalore tiles. The inner square is an open area for drying of clothes and common meeting place.

One of the royal houses, Kodial Guthu stands in the center of Mangalore city. The royal houses of Bunt are called Aramane.

The Kodagu district of Karnataka is the only region known for its martial people. Here, every Kodava belongs to a clan or Vokka. There are more than 300 clans in a community, and they lived within houses called Ain-Mane an ancestral house. Both the patriarch and the Matriarch lived in the Ain house with their families.

Wooden craft in a Vernacular building.

The Aynmane house has two massive columns at the entrance and has a central open courtyard. Men and women cultivated paddy on their lands and the bounty was shared after the harvest.

This ancestral house is market by a deeply cut passage called 'oni' leading to the front. Oni is paved with rough stones and has sloped walls on either side. An ideally built Ain Mane resembles a fort. This fort always represents the Kodava culture. The ancestral abode is a remarkable structure and a place for unique bonding. The structure of the building depicts the bonding of the family.

Typically, Ain Mane stands on a hillock surrounded by paddy fields, swaying area nut trees and coffee plantations.

Depending on the wealth of the family, it stands surrounded by the huts of the farmworkers and animal sheds. Well provides fresh water, it has sloping tiled roof to face the onslaught of torrential monsoon. The central courtyard opens to the sky. A narrow corridor runs all around the courtyard to connect all the rooms. The kitchen is at the rear end of the house to keep the smoke away whereas the toilet is always away from the main building.

There are always two massive wooden poles adorning the entrance. The central 'Naadubade' would consist of three wooden poles. The first pole is called as Kannikamba it supports the whole roof of Ainmane. It is as significant as the Thook Bolcha (hanging lamp) lit every day at the Nellaki Baade (prayer room). At the head of the family is called as karona, and is given the utmost importance. During ceremonies, the family members first touch base of Kannikamba to take blessing and then touch the feet of elders.

Images of sun, moon, flowers, on Kannikamba and main doors depict that Kodavas were nature worshipers. An integral part of Ainmane was Kaimada, which was an important structure building, built in then memory of the founder of the family. Unique feature about Kodava culture is that men and women share equal amount of respect, status, and position.

Padasale is the rectangular hall around which all rooms are arranged, Mundu is the inevitable open courtyard in the center. Kanni Kombara is the prayer place where a deity is installed. Kitchen, sacred, faced the east.

Vernacular Architecture of Andhra Pradesh

The state of Andhra Pradesh is known for its archeological remains and religious monuments. Andhra Pradesh is known for its Buddhist monuments such as Mahastupa and some more Hindu temples. The name of this state I heavily rooted in mythology and the name is also prevalent in Mahabharata.

Vernacular semi-open indoor spaces.

Most of the houses have single rectangular and linear form that depicts the typical architectural culture of the area. The houses are planned to minimize the heat loss or gain along with a little plantation area. There are benches made of Kadappa stone tiles and made and placed between two adjacent gates of the house. The space under the narrow staircase is used as storage area for household items. The flooring is done with Kadappa stones that are locally available and the foundation is also made with the same block stones.

The rectangular plan of the house is aligned along the north- south direction with entrance facing the south. The east and west compound walls are built that shade the house on each side. The overhanging and the projections further help in shading the underlying areas around the house.

The architecture of Andhra Pradesh is vast in a way that comprises Hindu, Islamic, and Buddhist architecture styles. It is the diverse richness of the state's architecture makes it one of the most coveted architectural destinations in India.

The Hindu Architecture

Sri Venkateshwara Temple and the Kalhateeswara temple are the oldest temples in the state that dates back to pre- Christian time. The state is adorned with architectural styles inspired by the Chalukyan, Dravidian, Nagara and the Orissa idiom. Tirupati is one of the most renowned temples in Andhra Pradesh.

The architecture of Venkataramana temple belongs to the Dravidian era, making the embellishments and engravings look finer. The pillars in the mandapa offer an illusion of space and create a graceful Indian rococo pattern.

Islamic Architecture

Hyderabad houses the Charminar, a magnificient Islamic structure. It is a 57 metre tall structure with latticework representing the time. Each Minar holds four stories, each floor marketed by an engraving ring around the minar. Charminar, with great aplomb, proclaims the architectural distinction with aspect and dignity. There are 12 tombs of Qutub Shahi Emperors existing outside the city walls. These tombs too reflect the Islamic style of the Deccan.

Buddhist Architecture

Andhra Pradesh has a massive legacy of Buddhist Architecture left behind. The village of Chexarla is home to many Buddhist shrines. The Kapotesheara temple, which was earlier a Bsuddhist temple was converted to a Hindu temple with a mandapa built in front of it. It has a Chaitya shrine with the chaitya window and Hindu sculptures seen on it.

The Amravati Stupa is famous for the Buddhist architectural of ancient India. It is constructed with brick and holds a circular vedica depicting Lord Buddha in a human form on an elephant. The stupa has elevated platforms that reach the height of 95ft projecting in four directions. This is an ideal example of Mauryan architecture in South India. The ruins of Nagarjunakonda also bear imperative features of Buddhist architecture.

Vernacular Architecture of Tamil Nadu

The most prominent vernacular architecture house of Tamil Nadu is the Chettinad house. These are ancestral houses of merchants of that time. The house primarily uses wood, what merchants traded with. Presently such houses are prevalent in some villages of Tamil Nadu .These are the kind of houses of the upper class in Tamil Nadu.

Vernacular Architecture of Pondicherry

Pondicherry was planned in two quarters, the one facing Bay of Bengal was for French and other was for native Tamilians. These two quarters were divided by a canal. The French quarters were built with French sensitivities in terms of its building and architecture. French quarters had bungalows on large plots and had institutional buildings.

The houses have unique character which is result of French influence on native Tamilian Architecture. The internal planning of the house is very traditional in nature, allowing people to live as per their will. The facades of these houses were designed with Greekcolumns and arched windows to present a colonial touch. The houses where columns are of greek design, courtyard inside is surrounded by the traditional wooden column. These unique houses are now termed as Franco- Tamilian houses. The influence of the French culture can also be seen in street art around the town and in décor of most houses.

Brahmin houses of Ambur

A type of vernacular houses come from the temple area where the houses are connected with temples. The houses are generally built of stones. As the people from this society are priests, it becomes comfortable as they are mostly just large pooja areas.

The vernacular houses of South India take into account the availability and are mostly connected to spirituality depicting the devotion of people of south of India.

The devotion of people is also prevalent through the numerous temples present throughout South India.

CHAPTER EIGHT

Appropriate Technology – Approach to Sustainable Development

Let's talk about the 'forefather' of Sustainable Development!

Appropriate technology is a movement (and its manifestations) encompassing technological choice and application that is small-scale, affordable by locals, decentralized, labor-intensive, energy-efficient, environmentally sustainable, and locally autonomous.

It was originally articulated as intermediate technology by the economist Ernst Friedrich "Fritz" Schumacher in his work Small Is Beautiful. Both Schumacher and many modern-day proponents of appropriate technology also emphasize the technology as people-centered.

Appropriate technology has been used to address issues in a wide range of fields. Well-known examples of appropriate technology applications include: bike- and hand-powered water pumps (and other self-powered equipment), the universal nut sheller, self-contained solar lamps and streetlights, and passive solar building designs.

Today, appropriate technology is often developed using open source principles, which have led to open-source appropriate technology (OSAT) and thus many of the plans of the technology can be freely found on the Internet. OSAT has been proposed as a new model of enabling innovation for sustainable development.

Appropriate technology is most commonly discussed in its relationship to economic development and as an alternative to technology transfer of more capital-intensive technology from industrialized nations to developing countries.

However, appropriate technology movements can be found in both developing and developed countries. In developed countries, the appropriate technology movement grew out of the energy crisis of the 1970s and focuses mainly on environmental and sustainability issues. Today the idea is multifaceted; in some contexts, appropriate technology can be described as the simplest level of technology that can achieve the intended purpose, whereas in others, it can refer to engineering that takes adequate consideration of social and environmental ramifications. The facets are connected through robustness and sustainable living.

Predecessors

Indian ideological leader Mahatma Gandhi is often cited as the "father" of the appropriate technology movement. Though the concept had not been given a name, Gandhi advocated for small, local and predominantly village-based technology to help India's villages become self-reliant. He disagreed with the idea of technology that benefited a minority of people at the expense of the majority, or that put people out of work to increase profit. In 1925 Gandhi founded the All-India Spinners Association and in 1935 he retired from politics to form the All-India Village Industries Association. Both organizations focused on village-based technology, similar to the future appropriate technology movement.

China also implemented policies similar to appropriate technology during the reign of Mao Zedong and the following Cultural Revolution. During the Cultural Revolution, development policies based on the idea of "walking on two legs" advocated the development of both large-scale factories and small-scale village industries.

E. F. Schumacher

Despite these early examples, Dr. Ernst Friedrich "Fritz" Schumacher is credited as the founder of the appropriate technology movement. A well-known economist, Schumacher worked for the British National Coal Board for more than 20 years, where he blamed the size of the industry's operations for its uncaring response to the harm black-lung disease inflicted on the miners. However it was his work with developing countries, such as India and Burma, which helped Schumacher form the underlying principles of appropriate technology.

Schumacher first articulated the idea of "intermediate technology," now known as appropriate technology, in a 1962 report to the Indian Planning Commission in which he described India as long in labor and short in capital, calling for an "intermediate industrial technology" that harnessed India's labor surplus. Schumacher had been developing the idea of intermediate technology for several years prior to the Planning Commission report. In 1955, following a stint as an economic advisor to the government of Burma, he published the short paper "Economics in a Buddhist Country," his first known critique of the effects of Western economics on developing countries. In addition to Buddhism, Schumacher also credited his ideas to Gandhi.

Initially, Schumacher's ideas were rejected by both the Indian government and leading development economists. Spurred to action over concern the idea of intermediate technology would languish, Schumacher, George McRobie, Mansur Hoda and Julia Porter brought together a group of approximately 20 people to form the Intermediate Technology Development Group (ITDG) in May 1965. Later that year, a Schumacher article published in The Observer garnered significant attention and support for the group. In 1967, the group published the Tools for Progress: A Guide to Small-scale Equipment for Rural Development and sold 7,000 copies. ITDG also created panels of experts and practitioners around specific technological needs (such as building construction, energy, and water) to develop intermediate technologies to address those needs. At a conference hosted by the ITDG in 1968 the term "intermediate technology" was discarded in favor of the term "appropriate technology" used today. Intermediate technology had been criticized as suggesting the technology was inferior to advanced (or high) technology and not including the social and political factors included in the concept put forth by the proponents. In 1973, Schumacher described the concept of appropriate technology to a mass audience in his influential work Small Is Beautiful: A Study of Economics As If People Mattered.

Growing trend

Between 1966 and 1975 the number of new appropriate technology organizations founded each year was three times greater than the previous nine years. There was also an increase in organizations focusing on applying appropriate technology to the problems of industrialized nations, particularly issues related to energy and the environment. In 1977, the OECD identified in its Appropriate Technology Directory 680 organizations involved in the development and promotion of appropriate technology. By 1980, this number had grown to more than 1,000. International agencies and government departments were also emerging as major innovators in appropriate technology, indicating its progression from a small movement fighting against the established norms to a legitimate technological choice supported by the establishment. For example, the Inter-American Development Bank created a Committee for the Application of Intermediate Technology in 1976 and the World Health Organization established the Appropriate Technology for Health Program in 1977.

Appropriate technology was also increasingly applied in developed countries. For example, the energy crisis of the mid-1970s led to the creation of the National Center for Appropriate Technology (NCAT) in 1977 with an initial appropriation of 3 million dollars from the U.S. Congress.

The Center sponsored appropriate technology demonstrations to "help low-income communities find better ways to do things that will improve the quality of life, and that will be doable with the skills and resources at hand." However, by 1981 the NCAT's funding agency, Community Services Administration, had been abolished. For several decades NCAT worked with the US departments of Energy and Agriculture on contract to develop appropriate technology programs. Since 2005, NCAT's informational web site is no longer funded by the US government.

Decline

In more recent years, the appropriate technology movement has continued to decline in prominence. Germany's German Appropriate Technology Exchange (GATE) and Holland's Technology Transfer for Development (TOOL) are examples of organizations no longer in operation. Recently, a study looked at the continued barriers to AT deployment despite the relatively low cost of transferring information in the internet age. The barriers have been identified as: AT seen as inferior or "poor person's" technology, technical transferability and robustness of AT, insufficient funding, weak institutional support, and the challenges of distance and time in tackling rural poverty.

A more free market-centric view has also begun to dominate the field. For example, Paul Polak, founder of International Development Enterprises (an organization that designs and manufactures products that follow the ideals of appropriate technology), declared appropriate technology dead in a 2010 blog post.

Polak argues the "design for the other 90 percent" movement has replaced appropriate technology. Growing out of the appropriate technology movement, designing for the other 90 percent advocates the creation of low-cost solutions for the 5.8 billion of the world's 6.8 billion population "who have little or no access to most of the products and services many of us take for granted."

Many of the ideas integral to appropriate technology can now be found in the increasingly popular "sustainable development" movement, which among many tenets advocates technological choice that meets human needs while preserving the environment for future generations. In 1983, the OECD published the results of an extensive survey of appropriate technology organizations titled, The World of Appropriate Technology, in which it defined appropriate technology as characterized by "low investment cost per work-place, low capital investment per unit of output, organizational simplicity, high adaptability to a particular social or cultural environment, sparing use of natural resources, low cost of final product or high potential for employment." Today, the OECD web site redirects from the "Glossary of Statistical Terms" entry on "appropriate technology" to "environmentally sound technologies." The United Nations' "Index to Economic and Social Development" also redirects from the "appropriate technology" entry to "sustainable development."

Potential resurgence

Despite the decline, several appropriate technology organizations are still in existence, including the ITDG which became Practical Action after a name change in 2005. Skat (Schweizerische Kontaktstelle für Angepasste

Technology) adapted by becoming a private consultancy in 1998, though some Intermediate Technology activities are continued by Skat Foundation through the Rural Water Supply Network (RWSN). Another actor still very active is the charity CEAS (Centre Ecologique Albert Schweitzer). A pioneer in food transformation and solar heaters, it offers vocational training in West Africa and Madagascar. There is also currently a notable resurgence as viewed by the number of groups adopting open source appropriate technology (OSAT) because of the enabling technology of the Internet. These OSAT groups include: Akvo Foundation, Appropedia, The Appropriate Technology Collaborative, Catalytic Communities, Centre for Alternative Technology, Center For Development Alternatives, Engineers Without Borders, Open Source Ecology, Practical Action, and Village Earth. Most recently ASME, Engineers Without Borders (USA) and the IEEE have joined together to produce Engineering for Change, which facilitates the development of affordable, locally appropriate and sustainable solutions to the most pressing humanitarian challenges.

Terminology

Appropriate technology frequently serves as an umbrella term for a variety names for this type of technology. Frequently these terms are used interchangeably; however, the use of one term over another can indicate the specific focus, bias or agenda of the technological choice in question. Though the original name for the concept now known as appropriate technology, "intermediate technology" is now often considered a subset of appropriate technology that focuses on technology that is more productive than "inefficient" traditional technologies, but less costly than the technology of industrialized societies. Other types of technology under the appropriate technology umbrella include:

1. **Capital-saving technology**
2. **Labor-intensive technology**
3. **Alternate technology**
4. **Self-help technology**
5. **Village-level technology**
6. **Community technology**
7. **Progressive technology**
8. **Indigenous technology**
9. **People's technology**
10. **Light-engineering technology**
11. **Adaptive technology**
12. **Light-capital technology**
13. **Soft technology**

A variety of competing definitions exist in academic literature and organization and government policy papers for each of these terms. However, the general consensus is appropriate technology encompasses the ideas represented by the above list. Furthermore, the use of one term over another in referring to an appropriate technology can indicate ideological bias or emphasis on particular economic or social variables. Some terms inherently emphasize the importance of increased employment and labor utilization (such as labor-intensive or capital-saving technology), while others may emphasize the importance of human development (such as self-help and people's technology).

It is also possible to distinguish between hard and soft technologies. According to Dr. Maurice Albertson and Audrey Faulkner, appropriate hard technology is "engineering techniques, physical structures, and machinery that meet a need defined by a community, and utilize the material at hand or readily available. It can be built, operated and maintained by the local people with very limited outside assistance (e.g., technical, material, or financial). it is usually related to an economic goal."

Albertson and Faulkner consider appropriate soft technology as technology that deals with "the social structures, human interactive processes, and motivation techniques. It is the structure and process for social participation and action by individuals and groups in analyzing situations, making choices and engaging in choice-implementing behaviors that bring about change."

A closely related concept is social technology, defined as "products, techniques and/or re-applicable methodologies developed in the interaction with the community and that must represent efective solution in terms of social transformation".

Practitioners

Some of the well known practitioners of the appropriate technology sector include:

1. **B.V. Doshi,**
2. **Buckminster Fuller,**
3. **William Moyer (1933–2002),**
4. **Amory Lovins,**
5. **Sanoussi Diakité,**
6. **Albert Bates,**
7. **Victor Papanek,**
8. **Giorgio Ceragioli (1930–2008),**
9. **Frithjof Bergmann,**

10. **Arne Næss, (1912–2009),**
11. **Mansur Hoda, and**
12. **Laurie Baker.**

Development

Schumacher's initial concept of intermediate technology was created as a critique of the currently prevailing development strategies which focused on maximizing aggregate economic growth through increases to overall measurements of a country's economy, such as gross domestic product (GDP). Developed countries became aware of the situation of developing countries during and in the years following World War II. Based on the continuing rise in income levels in Western countries since the Industrial Revolution, developed countries embarked on a campaign of massive transfers of capital and technology to developing countries in order to force a rapid industrialization intended to result in an economic "take-off" in the developing countries.

However, by the late 1960s it was becoming clear this development method had not worked as expected and a growing number of development experts and national policy makers were recognizing it as a potential cause of increasing poverty and income inequality in developing countries. In many countries, this influx of technology had increased the overall economic capacity of the country. However, it had created a dual or two-tiered economy with pronounced division between the classes. The foreign technology imports were only benefiting a small minority of urban elites. This was also increasing urbanization with the rural poor moving to urban cities in hope of more financial opportunities. The increased strain on urban infrastructures and public services led to "increasing squalor, severe impacts on public health and distortions in the social structure."

Appropriate technology was meant to address four problems: extreme poverty, starvation, unemployment and urban migration. Schumacher saw the main purpose for economic development programs was the eradication of extreme poverty and he saw a clear connection between mass unemployment and extreme poverty. Schumacher sought to shift development efforts from a bias towards urban areas and on increasing the output per laborer to focusing on rural areas (where a majority of the population still lived) and on increasing employment.

In developed countries

The term appropriate technology is also used in developed nations to describe the use of technology and engineering that result in less negative impacts on the environment and society, i.e., technology should be both environmentally sustainable and socially appropriate. E. F. Schumacher asserts that such technology, described in the book Small Is Beautiful, tends to promote values such as health, beauty and permanence, in that order.

Often the type of appropriate technology that is used in developed countries is "appropriate and sustainable technology" (AST), appropriate technology that, besides being functional and relatively cheap (though often more expensive than true AT), is durable and employs renewable resources.

Applications

Appropriate technologies find many applications in building and construction, agriculture, water and sanitation, energy generation and uses, transportation, health care, food preparation and storage, information and communication technologies, as well as finance.

Determining a sustainable approach

Features such as low cost, low usage of fossil fuels and use of locally available resources can give some advantages in terms of sustainability. For that reason, these technologies are sometimes used and promoted by advocates of sustainability and alternative technology.

Besides using natural, locally available resources (e.g., wood or adobe), waste materials imported from cities using conventional (and inefficient) waste management may be gathered and re-used to build a sustainable living environment. Use of these cities' waste material allows the gathering of a huge amount of building material at a low cost. When obtained, the materials may be recycled over and over in the own city/community, using the cradle to cradle design method. Locations where waste can be found include landfills, junkyards, on water surfaces and anywhere around towns or near highways. Organic waste that can be reused to fertilise plants can be found in sewages. Also, town districts and other places (e.g., cemeteries) that are subject of undergoing renovation or removal can be used for gathering materials as stone, concrete, or potassium.

Architects of the future, how appropriate is your technology?!

CHAPTER NINE

CASE Study

Various architects, planners and policymakers are working on a more sustainable building design for the betterment of societies of the future. The use of natural resources is being encouraged by substituting concrete, cement and energy-intensive materials with sun, water, wind and soil.

With the active growth of rural practices in a desire to have a convenient lifestyle, we are adopting some practices which are human-centric regardless of what damage has been done to the environment and exploiting its sources daily with knowing and unknowing facts. However, the aim is to address architects to include vernacular architecture in their contemporary construction methods with the acceptance of their clients.

The revival of vernacular architecture can be a direction to rural conservation and adaptation which also preserves what we already have for instance the potent to protect and enhance the natural environment and processes based on their historical, archaeological, and scientific interest, landscape, wildlife habitat, and cultural values also providing consistent agricultural use with the preservation of the area's respecting environmental and landscape values.

Villa in the Woods

Located between Bhimtal and Mukteshwar in the northern Indian state of Uttarakhand, the Villa in the Woods is part of a master plan designed to promote conscious community living amidst 90 acres of Himayalan forests of deodar, sal, oak, and rhododendron. With direct access from India's capital New Delhi, it lies in the Kumaon range of the Himalayas at an altitude of 6,700 feet. The brief for the masterplan development was centred around building a self-sufficient community in the hills, living in harmony with nature. The design scheme factors in detailed analyses of the existing terrain, slopes, vegetation, surface drainage patterns, and soil types. These studies were done to identify strategies for watershed management, stormwater management, and potential areas for development to minimize cut-and-fill and avoid disturbing the site's ecology.

With construction in the hills in India rapidly rising and damaging the sensitive terrain, the architects adhered to an eco-conscious sensibility. The architecture adopts pre-engineered technology with a structure composed of Light Gauge Framing Systems (LGSF) clad with locally-sourced materials. Mandating off-site construction, the architects leveraged a custom-designed modular system that uses lightweight mild steel sections and a six-layered drywall section, allowing the three-storey structures to be assembled at site from a kit of numbered pre-engineered parts. The construction uses a woven structural system akin to a basket weave, where structural integrity is derived from the composite whole as opposed to the strength of individual members. A narrative of age-old crafts skills developed with local artisans is superimposed on the primary shell.

Concrete piles and tie beams anchor the superstructure, whereas the dry construction methodology allows for a smooth and clinical construction process with nearly zero-waste generation. Therefore, the villa treads lightly on the ground, preventing damage to the slopes and surrounding trees and coexisting in harmony with the fragile ecology of which it is a part. Parameters integral to the project are:

Universal Access - The villa offers wheelchair accessibility and can be serviced by elevators. Wide boardwalks lead to the homes from access points, and all homes are directly accessible from the road.

Response to Terrain - Land parcels were demarcated according to gradient, sun exposure, scenery, and tree locations. The construction methodology adopted lends flexibility to bend the structures according to the site contours. The villa is raised on stilts to allow the flow of natural water streams. Brush layering, a bio-engineering method, was used to stabilize the slopes further, while stone-built gully plugs allow rainwater to percolate into the ground.

Building Lightly - The modular construction system employs minimal on-site wet work to cause the least disturbance to the site and surrounding ecology. It supports the efficient use of resources and energy with reduced water consumption and preserves the natural flow of water along the gradient. The plan for the villa follows the blueprint of nature, with each element sensitively charted out in congruence with the landscape. A dominant theme throughout is one of fluid transitions, removing the boundaries, and living with nature. Nestled amidst the dense foliage of deodar, chide, and oak trees, the villa is perched on stilts. Designed to evoke the experience of treehouse-living, the elevated structure is capped by a pitched roof and spacious balconies, offering residents solitude and direct connections with the lush outdoors.

The villa is split into three levels to offer differentiated experiences and uninterrupted lines of sight. Residents enter via a wooden boardwalk into the living quarters that also comprise a kitchen and dining area. A north-facing deck and a south-facing court promote outdoor lounging with panoramic vistas of the forests beyond. The floor above hosts bedrooms featuring floor-to-ceiling bay windows and skylights that frame expansive views of the landscape and fill interior spaces with daylight. The lowermost level houses the guest bedroom, staff quarters and ancillary facilities, merging with the gradient of the slope under the canopy of native vegetation.

The dining area doubles up as a conservatory, which, in addition to the sliding doors, window walls, and skylights, illuminates the interiors with daylight and enables residents to stargaze at night. The sun-drenched south court is strategically located to establish a seamless inside-outside experience and maximize views of the natural setting. The material palette of timber, slate, and local stone builds on the lexicon of koti-banal architecture, endemic to the Kumaon region. The interior design scheme further underpins the experience of being cocooned in a treehouse through its use of hand-crafted woodwork that blends classic notions of a simple wood structure with modernist angles, clean lines, and contemporary design elements.

Sustainability and energy-efficiency being paramount design concerns in an ecologically-sensitive context, the Villa in the Woods utilizes a range of measures to reduce its environmental impact. The integration of the native landscape, seasonal water bodies, and large tree cover ensure comfortable ambient temperatures for most of the year. The structure occupies a small footprint to minimize the impact on the existing terrain and trees. A hundred percent of the wastewater is treated through a phytorid-based system and is reused for horticulture among other purposes.

Through the incorporation of passive solar design and the use of vernacular building materials, the design simultaneously addresses aspects of daylight, natural ventilation, thermal comfort, and energy use. The building orientation and fenestration design ensure effective daylighting in all occupied spaces, reducing energy consumption to a minimum. Interior surfaces including the walls, floors, and the roof feature adequate insulation layers to regulate temperature and prevent heat loss during winters. Further, a radiant heating system is provided to **optimize thermal comfort and energy use.**

CHAPTER TEN

Relevance of this approach

The World doesn't need any more Star Architects.

If being Star Architect would mean all about imposing your own personal creative "Architectural Ego" on the people out there.

I believe that the basic intent of creativity should be to solve design problems, not to creatively force the realization of a heroic design ideal on the common mass.

We expect our buildings to be flexible and adaptable but fail to recognize that we, humans, are the most adaptable creature. Architecture may seem heavy and static and, therefore, may not be expected to be able to be changed too much without significant intervention.

Spend some time observing how Architecture reflects culture, and you'll get the sense that it's less of a profession and more of a world-view, a lens with which to interpret all of your surroundings. As such, it lends itself to so many visually creative mediums that call for the conceptualizing of space—graphic design, video production, film, etc.

I have always been fascinated watching people experience design in the world around them. I believe design functions like the sound of a ticking clock in the background we are not even fully aware of. It sends us subliminal messages into the innermost core of our brains, through an experiential journey of how to feel about it and what to expect.

Practicing and Preaching New Age Design Thinking and Sustainable Development, is the pathway to the future, which I want for all, became it offers a framework to generate economic growth, achieve social justice, exercise environmental stewardship and strengthen governance. Think Beyond Architecture.

Working with numerous other contemporaries and stalwarts in the domain of Architecture on projects across South Asia and beyond, I've come to closely appreciate those who trully understood Architectural design, both as a technical craft and an expressive medium, in an effort to creatively meet a certain challenge and building an experience. Today, since being an Architect has increasingly become a multidisciplinary effort, incorporating elements of technology, content and graphic design, the professional needs to experience and overcome challenges which are beyond mainstream Architecture.

Today's Architect should be a type of creator that's not easy to stereotype; Architects who THINK BEYOND ARCHITECTURE, having solutions beyond Architecture, because the world doesn't need traditional Architects or designers anymore. It needs Thought Leaders and Entrepreneurs and Business oriented helpful individuals, who are both open to accepting of the changes taking place in the broader world and empathetic to the people and industries being affected. The Architecture and design industries need people to provide a vision for what the technologically-driven future of experience can become.

Modern Architecture was born in 1920s to bring great Architecture to common people when Architecture was dominated by renaissance of classical and baroque Architecture only afforded by the bourgeois society (UNESCO, 1987).

The idea of bringing affordable Architecture by stripping off ornamentations and decorations was made possible by implementing formal compositions found in the emergence of abstract paintings into Architecture and providing playful and abundant daylight into buildings to promote health and well-being of the occupants.

Unfortunately, this great idea has been slowly eroded by the search for formalistic style. Modern Architecture has now become another exclusive Architectural style only afforded by the wealthy. It lost its touch with the rest of the society.

The upper 1 per cent can buy with their wealth, the bottom 5 per cent are taken care of by the government. The challenge for each Architect is to also serve the middle from the bottom 5 per cent to the upper 1 per cent.

I believe that, Architecture is not for selected few but for all. That is what I call Social Justice in Architecture.

Architecture be for Everyone.

I had been practicing and preaching in these lines for the past two decades across India and abroad, in close collaboration with many significant Government or Private Organizations of this industry, one of which is the famed Pegasus Design Solutions, AKA PDS, a Trademarked Brand Business Unit of the AskPEGASUS ADVISORY CONSULTANCY SERVICES OPC PRIVATE LIMITED, a Brand in its own rights, a collaboration of esteemed design minds, bringing in expertise across various domains beyond geographical barriers, serving throughout South Asia and beyond, in seamless harmony with an array of highly significant project experiences.

"Design and innovation is our way of life, our point of view." – Team Pegasus.

Pegasus Design Solutions, as a part of the group, collaborates boldly to create, problem solve and try new ideas in designing places that people have loved & appreciated since 1999, working with the approach to bring this idea of Architecture be for Everyone back to its track to provide great Architecture for all people. Instead of using mundane formal compositions in designing, PDS believes in establishing abstract conceptual idea combined with careful attention to context, materials, detailing, cost, function, and pragmatism as the guiding forces toward great Architecture through responsible creativity, with the motive of:

Being purposeful about accessibility and collaboration; breaking new grounds and changing the traditional industrial practices.

Being fully vested in every project, matching the client's passion by sharing their vision with empathy.

Being nimble and unconventional, approaching every project with a streamlined research oriented methodology, no matter the size.

Pegasus Design Solutions strives to take green Architectural approach beyond minimizing the embodied energy, energy usage of the building, site impact and other sustainable strategies through PDS. PDS takes it further into ease of maintenance, operating costs, culture and habits of the occupants, and even energy and cost of designing. Saving energy comes hand in hand with maintainability and operation of the building, understanding the client's perspective that ease of maintenance and operation are very important design considerations to the long-term success of the sustainability goals of a project, and that's what PDS strives to achieve every time in a project, by Design.

- Website: *https://pegasusorg.com*
- Facebook Page: *https://www.facebook.com/pegasusorg*
- Email: *customer.pds@gmail.com*
- Helpline/WhatsApp: *+91 6289 810812*

Striving to involve the whole complex of visual communications: talent, creative ability, manual skill, and technical knowledge, Pegasus Design Solutions works around Aesthetics and economics, technology and psychology, because they are intrinsically related to all its processes. AskPEGASUS ADVISORY CONSULTANCY SERVICES OPC PRIVATE LIMITED is always motivated to out-service the clients' expectations and protect and promote their vision every step of the way. AskPEGASUS ADVISORY CONSULTANCY SERVICES OPC PRIVATE LIMITED works with a unique 100 per cent employee-owned structure, which means that everyone in its working team is 100 per cent committed towards the holistic success of the projects in hand.

Pegasus Design Solutions has the mission to assertively harness out of the box concepts and enthusiastically reinvent highest standards of future proof designs on the go by a dignified profession of creativity, cultivating opportunities with potentials and proficiency while aspiring for an infinite exposure to the brighter and the better. PDS is uniquely hands-on, and its transparent approach puts relationships first, not egos.

Committed to improving the community, AskPEGASUS ADVISORY CONSULTANCY SERVICES OPC PRIVATE LIMITED is relentlessly engaged in making it sustainable by focusing on long lasting partnerships and repeat clients, since 1999.

It is my sincere hope that AskPEGASUS ADVISORY CONSULTANCY SERVICES OPC PRIVATE LIMITEDwould use every client's resources responsibly, not only to save money but also to make them available to be used for others in need. Because, I believe that we should seek to bring social justice to Architecture by considering those who do not have voice in design but interact with Architecture, such as passersby, visitors, and children, to ensure they are heard, all the people out there.

The best Architecture is created through a shared vision between client, community and Architect that is garnered through listening, evaluation and leadership. Heightening the spatial and visual literacy and assisting in this process, Pegasus Group strives to enliven the public discussion and equip future Architects with a broad frame of reference that assures aspirational Architecture is created for everyone. I hope the future Architect's will want to be a part of it.

I Practice what I Preach.

Personally, the focus of my Architectural journey had been problem solving of social and user issues, in addition to environmental issues, faced by Architecture and its context, that is to say, it is not to satisfy my own personal Heroic Architectural Ego, but to create what works for the people, and what looks and feels good in composition and context for them, by Design.

It is my sincere desire to extend all available resources to provide affordable Architecture and Education to those out there in need, in collaboration with those who share our beliefs for the greater good.

A New-Age Book can no longer remain as a passive disposition of someone's enlightenment. It has to be interactive. Like it or not.

Therefore, please do go back to any of my Social Media Pages and connect with me, should you require any such support, anytime, ever. Let's work together for a greater good!

I believe that truly great Architecture should be selfless. It should not be self-serving but about making designs that are in harmony with human nature and respect the integrity, context and tradition of each context. It is all about a New Age Design Thinking.

The New Age Design Thinking

Today it has become important for mainstream Architects to 'Delete' their traditional limitations and 'Install' a New Age Design Thinking, which is essentially about exploring a multilayered structured processes that encourage new age innovation and creativity in problem solving. It's a useful approach for cities that want to design meaningful solutions to city challenges by working with their citizens and ultimately aim to become "SMART".

"Good design is like a refrigerator—when it works, no one notices, but when it doesn't, it sure stinks." –Irene Au

New Age Design Thinking allows for the user of the system to have a more structured plan for understanding innovation and to grow more as a company. New Age Design Thinking is thus a solution-focused, problem-solving methodology that helps companies, and individuals alike to get a desired outcome on an inner problem, or to work forward on a future plan.

As Roger Martin, author of Design of Business, Put it:

"Design-thinking firms stand apart in their willingness to engage in the task of continuously redesigning their business...to create advances in both innovation and efficiency — the combination that produces the most powerful competitive edge."

Businesses that create smart city solutions using supplier-centered design are often surprised when their products or services are not popular among city governments or citizens. They have often failed to seek out and understand the real needs of their users. Increasingly, design processes that place the citizen at the center are recognized as being critical to the creation of successful smart solutions.

The process of design thinking basically has five stages that focus on creating and testing a solution; through the process you continue to learn and improve upon initial ideas (Stanford Design Program and the Standard Arts Institute, 2012).

Empathize: work with the user to fully understand their experience of the problem that needs to be solved by observation, interaction and immersion.

Define: work through the outputs of the empathize stage to form a user point of view that will be addressed in the solution design.

Idea: explore lots of ideas and generate a wide range of possible solutions.

Prototype: transform an idea into a simple version of the solution ready for testing.

Test: trial the solution, use feedback to re-consider earlier stages, improve the solution and test again.

5-Stage Model by Hasso-Plattner Institute of Design, Stanford - Today more and more industries than ever are taking a human-centric approach to evolving their existing products and generating new ideas to serve their customers better.

This Five stage model was originally proposed by the Hasso-Plattner Institute of Design at Stanford, and it is continually used by individuals and firms to better innovate their selves. Let's Dive Deep into the details and try to understand further.

"The alternative to good design is always bad design. There is no such thing as no design." –Adam Judge

Empathize

The first stage of Design Thinking is called Empathize. This stage is meant to get a better understand of the problem that you wish to conquer. This includes: consulting experts of the matter, engaging farther into the issue to better understand the problem at hand, as well as working the issue though as a group to have a deeper comprehension of everything that is involved with the problem.

The Empathy stage allows for Design Thinkers to gain insight into the needs regarding the issue along with setting aside their personal assumptions regarding it. A substantial amount of information is gathered during the Empathize stage and is carried on to the next few stages to help define the problem and understand how to deal with it.

Define

The second stage of Design Thinking is called Define. During this stage in the Design Thinking process you are putting together all the information you gained during the Empathize step. Essentially, you will analyze your data and put them in order to better concrete the problems that your team has defined to this point.

The Define stage will help your team gather great ideas and be able to understand how to use them effectively. From here, you and your team will start to progress into the third stage of Design thinking, Ideate.

Ideate

The third stage of Design Thinking is called Ideate. During this stage, Design thinkers start to use the information from the previous stages to generate logical ideas. From here, your team will start to make ideas that may be "out of the box" or perhaps just ideas that may normally skipped over when not all of information is presented. This stage allows for an alternative way to solve normalized problems.

By the end of this phase, your team should have a few ideas to solve the problem. It's important during this phase that your team should generate a lot of ideas just so you have many to choose from when starting the next phase in the Design Thinking process, Prototype.

Prototype

The fourth stage of Design Thinking is called Prototype. During this stage the team will work on creating a number of inexpensive products with specific features. This allows for the Design Thinkers to investigate possible solutions to the problems that were identified the earlier stages of the Design Thinking process. With each new prototype, the team investigates different aspects of the problem and explores how each of the prototypes would fix the problem.

By the end of this stage, the Design Thinkers should have a better understanding of the constraints they are apparent of the prototype. This is also allowing for the team to the problems that would be created by each prototype, and how they could fix the prototype to make the prototype inherently better. From here, the team should be ready to move on to the final step of the Design Thinking process, Test.

Test

The fifth and final stage of Design Thinking is called Test. During this stage Design Thinkers test their prototypes made in stage four. They test their prototypes to see how well they solve/handle the problem that they initially analyzed in stages one and two. Even during this step, the team can and will make alterations and refinements in order to make the product more polished for their needs.

With this process, it allows for your team to go back to previous stages and revise their information to get the best outcomes for their end product. Essentially, the team can continue to do this until they are either solving their problem, or until they are satisfied with their product.

"The role of the designer is that of a good, thoughtful host anticipating the needs of his guests" –Charles Eames

New Age Design Thinking in Smart city solutions (products or services) can come in handy using a variety of design approaches.

Supplier-centered design – a designer creates a solution they think cities or citizens need.

User-centered design – a designer shapes a solution to the user's point of view.

Co-design – a designer works with stakeholders to help them design a solution for themselves.

Co-production – a designer works with stakeholders to produce a solution.

Co-creation – this is where co-design and co-production are brought together. Citizens work in partnership with a designer to co-create solutions.

New Age Design Thinking is a flexible process that is solution-focused to help solve problems that everyday people have issues with, crucial in envisaging a Smart City.

I have published detailed articles on this particular topic and beyond; go back to my Social Media Pages and check it out sometime!

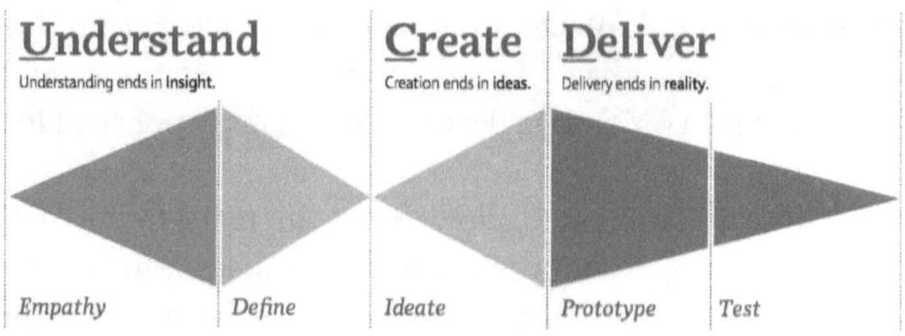

UNDERSTAND | CREATE | DELIVER

Well-designed spaces are not just a matter of taste or a question of aesthetics; they literally shape our ideas about who we are and what we deserve. Design impacts our health, our education, our community, our sense of self-worth, and more, yet all-too-often design is viewed as a luxury. To address critical problems of access and inequity at home and around the world, good design must transcend the endless coverage of multi-million dollar homes and Silicon Valley office spaces to become a key means of uplifting those who need it most.

I have always believed that Architecture should be about creating spaces for people to live their best lives, and not a profession which is largely disconnected from the people most directly impacted by its work. I think Architecture should not be an elitist profession, seemingly unconcerned with some of the greatest needs in the world, but start by catering to the relatively simple needs of the common public.

Architecture like art can change how we look at the world; it can inspire, surprise, alarm, delight, and our relationship with it can change with time and familiarity. Unlike other art forms, Architecture must also operate on both a functional and practical level, with technical demands such as weatherproofing, structural stability, and regulatory controls coming into play.

Quality Architecture is about meeting these practical demands while creating spaces that are poetic and human.

The experience of being in buildings that successfully negotiate the tension between practicality and delight is memorable and enlightening. Architecture is a socially-engaged art form and consequentially has an impact on us all in some way or another. It doesn't exist for its own good but instead must address political, social, environmental and economic imperatives. It must also engage with the world of ideas, of culture and imagination.

Although COVID-19 has devastated the world in so many ways, the bright side of it shows that human activities do impact the environment and that nature is capable of self-healing. We see this in the evidence of lower pollution numbers in our air and water. It also proves that we can work remotely, consume less, commute less, and focus on meaningful human interactions on levels which were beyond our mainstream understanding until now. We have learned our lesson and, when we are out of this pandemic, we should retain those good habits to make the world a better place in the future.

Vernacular Architecture is known for its use of local materials and knowledge of material combination without any supervision of a professional architect. The term Vernacular Architecture means, 'domestic,native,indigenous'. Many tribal settlements and traditional building represent vernacular architecture for eg. Wada Housing in Maharashtra, Bhonga Housing in Gujarat, Toda Tribal Hut in Nilgiri Mountains etc. Vernacular architecture is functional, informal and designed mostly with mud and bamboo.

Some of the common characteristics of vernacular architecture comprise:

Orientation: Different orientations of the building produce favourable thermal conditions in the building.

Shading: A building, including its external walls and its openings, gets exposed to sun and water. In vernacular architecture, the overhanging eaves do away with this by providing protection.

Ventilation: The relative humidity of the building is regulated by cross-ventilation. This is primarily important for huts located in hot and humid climates.

Some of the factors like form and massing, spatial organization and open and built distribution help to control the overall performance of the building.

Climate Responsive: Vernacular architecture includes a traditional design which is climatically responsive and aesthetically pleasing. But traditional architecture is different from the vernacular, though they are inter-related. It is a climate-responsive design, built to lower the environmental impact, thereby reducing energy consumption.

Typical Features of Vernacular Architecture

Plinth: It is the lowest part of the vernacular hut.

Walls: The walls used are mostly load-bearing structures except for the fact that they are wooden framed structures.

Openings: To maintain the thermal balance, the vernacular huts have minimum possible openings.

Roofs: They do not end touching the wall, but project outwards creating a large overhanging in order to protect the wall from sunlight and rain. They are usually sloping in form and their pitch varies according to the wind speed of that area.

Loft: It is the overhead storage in the built structure. This loft space separates the upper hot zone from the lower cool zone of the building.

Elements of Vernacular Architecture

Water: It is the most important resource which has to be utilized cautiously. For this, there are strategies like water harvesting and recycling which have to be adopted.

Structural Longevity: The materials used in the building decide the life cycle of the building. The materials that cost more and consume more energy and resource in their manufacturing can be used to generate more benefits basis their recycling potentials and disposal.

Light and Ventilation: The climate responsive buildings reduce consumption of artificial lighting and air conditioning systems.

Technology: The technologies through features like jails, fountains, water to cool building fabrics, etc. add sustainable features at a macro level.

Today,as the demand for sustainable architecture increases many architects and designers are investing their time and resources to decode the world of vernacular architecture around the world, so to merge traditional outlooks with modern techniques

Let us look at the things Architects Should Learn From Vernacular Architecture as a subject:

1. Co-existence

Architecture is not just about filling the site with steel blocks or construction concrete rather it's about understanding the place with consideration of its social, cultural, and environmental essence. Contrary to traditional architecture, the architectural space in contemporary architecture depends on an artificial urban landscape to harmonize and rationalize it with the individuality of contemporary buildings. Cities are full of landmarks rather than co-existed urban form. Whereas traditional architecture was harmonious with the surrounding, climate, geography, landscape and human psychology along with successfully co-existing, treating architecture as a holistic natural living element, stand still yet function, similar to trees as an organic living environment inventory with judicious use of building material, form and technology.

2. Local materials

The vernacular architecture was designed in direct response to the locally available material such as bamboo, thatch, sticks, mud, or grass for construction, which were more energy-efficient, cheap, affordable, easily available, and even required less labour. The building construction material used today is more synthetic, not sustainable, and hard to reuse such as concrete and steel. The building industry consumes immense energy and contributes majorly to the world's greenhouse gas emission.

3. Construction methods

Traditional architecture still exists today and proved to more durable in comparison to modern architecture. The use of local material allowed easy extraction, easy preparation, and the possibility of creating composite which permitted thermal efficiency, recyclability, biodegradability, and sustainability. The construction method was changed on trial and error basis and material for construction was changed or added depending on the survival of the building. The vernacular architecture was the result of those attempts to create the best suitable building according to the context.

4. Sustainability

Vernacular buildings around the world are a great example of sustainable solutions to building problems. The buildings were energy-efficient and highly sustainable due to the use of local material and building technology. The architecture was in deep harmonization with site surrounding and had a minimal environmental impact as the most commonly used building material were mud and earth, which improved the building's thermal and acoustic performance and enhanced the sustainability aspects. The construction was done on sustainable principles using local materials and technology through the amalgamation of the physical and natural environment with cultural, social, and mystical values offering rational solutions to the harsh climate and human needs.

5. Culture

Each community had its style of architecture, that featured their main character, culture, and retrieved a sense of heritage, giving them a unique appearance. They cannot be separated from the culture they were developed in, resulting in their own regional and economical aesthetic. The houses are built according to their regional possibilities, needs, availability of materials, topography, and climate. Traditional buildings that were rich for their culture have lost their identity due to the influence of Western culture which led to the construction of buildings that were internationally acceptable and used similar material across the globe.

6. Climate Responsive

The glass and steel architecture constructed all over the world ignores the specific climate of the place and is left at the mercy of the climate. The buildings are fully air-conditioned and require year-round air conditioning contrary to the natural cooling options used by vernacular buildings which consumed less energy. These buildings prove to be inefficient, where glass exterior traps the sun's rays during summer and haemorrhages heat throughout the winter.

7. A contextual approach to design

A building's fundamental purpose is to provide a comfortable living environment, protected from the extremes of climate, as well as respond to the site, setting, and context. The construction style of each vernacular style differs according to the context of the site. For example; the traditional buildings of North-Eastern India are constructed over varying topography consisting of plains, mountains, and frequent flood-affected areas, using bamboo which is found in great abundance in the North-Eastern region; Giant houses built in Fujian, China from the 12th – 19th century with the main purpose of prevention against the plunder and attack of the outside forces, constructed strong fortress using locally available material that protected inhabitants from the outside dangers.

8. Expandable form and space

Architecture should be capable of growing according to the changing needs of the inhabitants. The form which easily accepts change and process-based incremental growth. Vernacular architecture had the potential to accommodate such changes in its spatial layout. For example, the traditional Malay house, the Bumbung Panjang, could easily allow an addition to the house on the simple roof in an efficient way.

9. Building Image

All the buildings of a particular vernacular style looked similar due to the use of the same material, color, and technique of construction. There was a sense of equality among people living in such dwellings which were achieved through the outside building image. All buildings seemed equal and there was a less visible difference between rich and poor from the outside.

I strongly believe that New-Age Architecture should have the unique ability to dignify people.

It should make people feel valued, respected, honored and seen in ways never imagined. Architecture be for Everyone.

The Happy Readers Club

Join the Happy Readers Club and celebrate your success story!!!

"Without investment there will not be growth, and without growth there will not be employment." - Muhtar Kent

"Young people entering the job market seek employment at companies with values that match theirs." - Neil Blumenthal

"Choose a job you love, and you will never have to work a day in your life." — Confucius

"It's time to start living the life we've imagined." —Henry James

Technical Abbreviations

ADB - Asian Development Bank

APEDA - Agricultural & Processed Food Products Export Development Authority

BARC - Baba Atomic Research Centre

BCW - Backward Classes Welfare

BDO - Block Development Officer

BIS - Bureau of Indian Standards

BMW - Bio Medical Waste

BOP - Business Optimization Plan

CBMWTF - Common Biomedical Waste Treatment Facility

CESC - Calcutta Electric Supply Corporation

CETP - Common Effluent Plant

CFA - Central Finance Assistance

CH - Correctional Home

CHC - Community Health Centre

CHWTSDF - Common Hazardous Waste Treatment Storage and Disposal Facility

CIDCO - City and Industrial Development Corporation Limited

CPWA - Central Public Works Accounts

CPWD - Central Public Works Department

CWC - Central Warehousing Corporation

DBFOT - Design-Build-Finance-Operate-Transfer

DCR - Development Control Regulation

DFC - Dedicated Freight Corridor

DMD - Dahej Manufacturing Division

DNEPL - Dahej Nagothane Ethane Pipeline

GDCR - General Development Control Regulation

GoI - Government of India

GoWB - Government of West Bengal
GP - Gram Panchayat
GSB - Granular Sub-base
GSDP - Gross State Domestic Product
H&FW - Health & Family Welfare
HCC - Heritage Conservation Committee
HDPE - High-Density Poly Ethylene
HMD - Hazira Manufacturing Division
HW - Hazardous Waste
IIA - Integrated Industrial Area
INC - Incineration
IPHS - Indian Public Health Standard
IR - Inspection Report
IT - Information Technology
JNNURM - Jawaharlal Nehru National Urban Renewal Mission
JPI - Joint Physical Inspection
Kg/Hr - Kilogram per hour
KMC - Kolkata Municipal Corporation
KMDA - Kolkata Metropolitan Development Authority
KMRCL - Kolkata Metro Rail Corporation Limited
kV - Kilo volt
LIFO - Last In First Out
LPCD - Litres per Capita per Day
MCM - Million cubic metre
MLD - Million liters per day
MMC - Multimodal Corridor
MMR - Mumbai Metropolitan Region
MMTPA - Million Metric Tonnes Per Annum
MNRE - Ministry of New and Renewable Energy
MoEF - Ministry of Environment & Forest
MoRD - Ministry of Rural Development
MOU - Memorandum of Understanding

MoUD - Ministry of Urban Development

MSME - Ministry of Micro Small and Medium Enterprises

MSW - Municipal Solid Waste

MT - Metric Ton

MW - Megawatt

MWML - Mumbai Waste Management Limited

NABARD - National Bank for Agriculture and Rural Development

NBC - National Building Code

NeGP - National e-Governance Plan

NGO - Non-Governmental Organization

NH - National Highway

NHAI - National Highways Authority of India

NKDA - New Town Kolkata Development Authority

NMMC - Navi Mumbai Municipal Corporation

NMSCIL - Navi Mumbai Smart City Infrastructure Limited

NOX - Nitrogen oxide

P&RD - Panchayat & Rural Development

PCB - Pollution Control Board

PHE - Public Health Engineering

RDF - Refuse derived fuel

REC - Rural Electrification Corporation

RGPL - Reliance Gas Pipelined Limited

RIL - Reliance Industries Limited

RSPM - Respirable suspended particulate matter

SH - State Highway

SLF - Sanitary Landfill

SO2 - Sulphur dioxide

SPA - Special Planning Authority

SPV - Special Purpose Vehicle

STP - Sewage treatment plant

SWOT - Strengths, Weaknesses, Opportunities, and Threats

TCM - Thousand cubic meters

TPA - Tons per annum

TPH - Tons per hour

TTC - Trans Thane Creek

ULB - Urban local body

USP - Unique Selling Proposition

V - Voltage

WBFES - West Bengal Fire & Emergency Services

WBM - Water Bound Macadam

WBMSCL - West Bengal Medical Services Corporation Limited

WBSCS - West Bengal State Council of Sports

WBSMB - West Bengal State Marketing Board

WBPCB - West Bengal Pollution Control Board

WBSR - West Bengal Service Rules

WBSRDA - West Bengal State Rural Development Agency

WBSRLM - West Bengal State Rural Livelihoods Mission

WBSWC - West Bengal State Warehousing Corporation

WBTR - West Bengal Treasury Rules

WBUHS - West Bengal University of Health Sciences

WC - Water Closet

WDRA - Warehousing Development & Regulatory Authority

WHO - World Health Organization

WTP - Water Treatment Plant

ZP - Zilla Parishad

Epilogue

I sincerely believe that an Architect should always be a student, constantly learning, because there is a lot to learn.

And I understand that continuous learning should be a process of learning new skills and knowledge on an on-going basis, lifelong.

Learning is essential to our existence. Just like food nourishes our bodies, information and continued learning nourishes our minds. Lifelong learning is an indispensable tool for every career and organization. Today, continuous learning forms a necessary part in acquiring critical thinking skills and discovering new ways of relating to people from different cultures. To live a life without continuous learning is unthinkable.

"The only thing that is constant is change," -Heraclitus famously said.

I have experienced it the hard way. Always change is there in your career, change is there in your personal life, change is there in your community and organizations. One of the most effective ways of dealing with change is lifelong learning.

Continuous learning is your self-motivated persistence in acquiring knowledge and competencies in order to expand your skill set and develop future opportunities. It forms part of your personal and professional development in an effort to avoid stagnation and reach your full potential.

Learning can come in many forms, from formal course taking, to casual social learning. It involves self-initiative and taking on challenges. Continuous learning can also be within an organization, or it can be personal, such as in lifelong learning. I honestly believe that:

The more you Learn, the more you can Earn!

In my experience, the following benefits of lifelong learning should be reason enough to never stop learning.

Be market relevant: Don't be left behind, ensuring you remain relevant to your sector by keeping yourself up-to-date with latest trends and adapting to new age skills. In order to function effectively in this technology driven rapidly changing world, you need to keep learning new things to remain valuable in the industry.

Be ready for challenge: Lifelong learning helps you quickly adapt to unexpected changes, because, by continuing to learn, you will more easily step out of your comfort zone and take new opportunities head on.

Be Smart in your career: When you are always learning, you will keep improving, and you will grow in your career, and start to receive recommendations from colleagues and managers. This is important because in today's world, chances are that you will switch jobs multiple times throughout your life and you will be in need of new skills and new recommendations regularly.

Be confident with competence: Learning new things gives us confidence, we feel accomplished in our own unique competence and we feel better ready to take on more new challenges and explore new ventures.

Be a Smart ideator: Acquiring new skills unveils new opportunities and helps us find simple solutions to difficult problems, and even help us earn more money.

Be open-minded: Continuous learning opens your mind and changes your attitude, because the more you learn, the better you'll get at seeing more sides of a situation, helping you understand the situation more deeply and resolve it more easily.

Be a mentor: Frankly, continuous learning isn't just about you, it helps develop your leadership skills which then translate into fostering lifelong learning in other individuals, by encouraging them to pursue further education.

Massive knowledge leads to massive Humility. Intellectual humility is the owning of one's cognitive limitations, a healthy recognition of one's intellectual debts to others, and low concern for intellectual domination and certain kinds of social status. Because, being humble means not being proud or arrogant, and not thinking you're better than other people. It is important that rather than focusing on yourself – on your own accomplishments or your own self-interest – you put other people's needs and feelings first.

"The more I learn, the more I realize how much I don't know." — Albert Einstein

Knowledge is now at everyone's fingertips. Those not making use of this opportunity will remain where they are and their capabilities diminishing in importance. Therefore a lifelong learning attitude is even more important for an Architect of the future.

Too much to explore, but too little time!

I believe that Architecture is unique among other creative and artistic professions; because Architecture must always reflect the age and cultural context that produced it. Designing and Building Architecture takes time, money, and collaboration (from financiers, civic officials, builders, Architects, and more). It doesn't happen in a vacuum and can never truly have just one 'Author'. Architects work in a team, with dozens if not hundreds or thousands of people to shape their buildings, and along this chain, a deeper and richer set of values are transmitted; ones that define exactly how cultures see themselves and their world, and also how people see and experience each other.

The more I Teach, the more I Learn!

Beyond merely providing shelter, Architecture becomes the centre stage set in context for our lives. It's the reason Architects feel empowered, connected and thriving in a busy public plaza, and humbled in a soaring monumental manifestation of Architecture. Communities form within, at the behest of Architecture, and take on their buildings' characteristics. Architecture connects to economics and the sciences, and the people who practice it should both be detail-oriented technicians, as well as poets of space and form.

Architects play a spearheading role in creating smart urban spaces and cities as a whole. Cities become engines of growth for the economy of every nation, including India. Nearly 31 per cent of India's current population lives in urban areas and contributes 63 per cent of India's GDP (Census 2011). With increasing urbanization, urban areas are expected to house 40 per cent of India's population and contribute 75 per cent of India's GDP by 2030 (MoUD, 2015). This requires comprehensive development of physical, institutional, social and economic infrastructure. All are important in improving the quality of life and attracting people and investments to the City, setting in motion a virtuous cycle of growth and development. Development of Smart Cities is a step in that direction.

It is important to understand that our desperation can become our inspiration at the times of utmost crisis, which is now.

"As we express our gratitude, we must never forget that the highest appreciation is not to utter words but to live by them." — John F. Kennedy

I believe we should be rising up above and beyond any ideological differences, and working for the betterment of the people and the planet, and be thankful to various corporations and Government authorities who are trying to help our civilization to progress with a genuinely honest intent.

The idea of having a Net-Zero emission city is not too far away from becoming reality. The future Smart City will include a host of clean energy sources to power its city. Energy in smart cities is efficient, using less energy because of the constant real-time data collection and analysis

The Devil is in the details - the more you seek, the more it hides!

As the world becomes increasingly interconnected and technology-dependent, a new wave of smart applications is changing how we approach everyday activities. Utility appliances such as intelligent fridges, personal AI assistants or smart home security applications create opportunities for more efficient living. While the ideas of "Smart Cities" have been proposed as the future of urbanism, the question remains: how do we connect our new age technologies for the ultimately "efficient" society of the future?

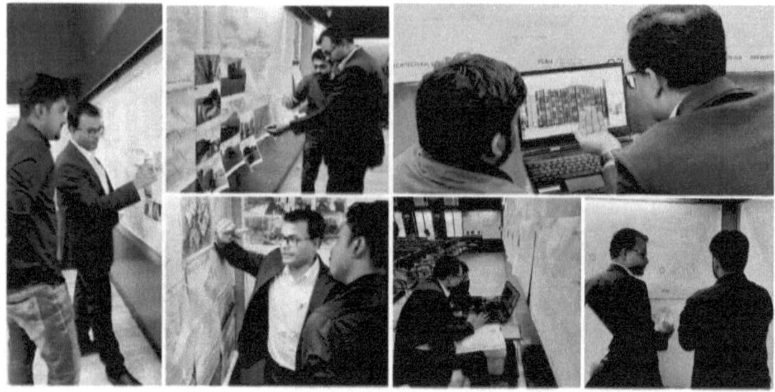

Teaching & Learning had always been a TWO-WAY process for me.

In continuation to what I had talked about in details in my previous Book of the same series, let us understand very clearly that the future Smart Cities will bring together infrastructure and technology to improve the quality of life of citizens and enhance their interactions with the urban environment. But how can data from areas such as public transport, air quality meters and energy production be integrated and effectively used?

Could we therefore identify what future proof solutions should we focus on?

Combat poverty by promoting economic development and job creation,

Involve local community in local government,

Reduce air pollution by upgrading energy use and alternative transport systems,

Create private-public partnerships to provide services such as waste disposal and housing,

Plant trees and incorporate the care of city green spaces as a key element in urban planning, and so on.

As I keep emphasizing over and over again, that a New-Age Book can no longer remain as a passive disposition of someone's enlightenment, but must be interactive.

Therefore, I would request you to please do go to any of my Social Media Pages and type in your Views, your Comments, your Thoughts, on this particular concept. Let me hear you out, what your feeling is about this New-Age Book of mine.

I will get back to you!

"Alone we can do so little; together we can do so much."
- Helen Keller

It is pertinent to mention here as an honest disclaimer which I had always believed, is in the fact that creating such a Book is no less than creating any Architectural Project in its true essence. Because just like any Architectural Project, this book too had involved a highly meticulous and painstaking process of putting together years of well researched and well crafted and relevant excerpts, created/ adopted wholly or in parts, from my personally copyrighted database, as well as from various other freely available literature, graphics and allied relevant open to public resources which are accessible throughout the world wide web, wherein due credit/ courtesy is hereby being openly acknowledged/ referenced to the original authors/ pioneers thereof. When you have nothing to hide, nothing to lose and nothing to prove – Humility is yours for sure!

Let Practicing and Preaching go hand in hand..!!

This book is the outcome of my extensive due diligence and Research and Development over several years of personal work experience and introspections gained directly through Industry-Academia interfacing, and therefore I believe that such a knowledge base can only grow over time and space, and may not be contested for literary uniqueness and/ or conclusiveness on the stated subject, and therefore the readers are advised to freely explore/ research on their own, should there be any further personal academic clarifications required. This book is published and shared through this print/ digital medium to my students and to whosoever be interested, for the sole purpose of academic interest and reference to the beginners of this subject for their study/ research activity only, with the benevolent intent of sharing my decades of first-hand knowledge as widely and as affordably as plausible to the world in all good faith. I believe that human evolution has two predominant stages - from being somebody to being nobody; and from being nobody to being everybody. If you want to lift yourself up, try to lift up someone else. Because at the end of the day - Sharing is Caring!

And finally to wrap up the concepts, as far as my Architectural introspection goes, I believe that there are immense opportunities for Architects in the future. At present, only around 1.2 lakh architects are in India and there is a huge demand for new Architects and building designers in near future. Because in India, with the vision of 100 smart cities and many new projects, future possibilities and prospectus for Architects are very bright.

Architecture is the only discipline which has 100 % employability - only if you know how!

With the rapid evolution of available technologies and the integration of them into the profession, the role of an Architect is changing faster than it ever has before. With the rapid evolution of available technologies, latest software and the integration of new techniques in buildings, a career as an architect and the role of an architect is changing faster than it ever has before. What had never ever been thought before is becoming the New Normal and Architects of the future would probably have to explore ways to integrate their services through BIG Data analytics, or through Blockchain Technology, or through Machine Learning, or through Cloud Computing.

Architects are basically problem-solvers and designers of many aspects of human life, and that is the reason why Architects can be employable almost anywhere. Architects can explore to work with development organizations wherein they are approached to provide their specialized services and expertise. A large portion of unexplored opportunities in engineering design, research and consultancy comes up in Government associations, for example, Public Works Department, the Archeological Department, Ministry of Defense, National Building Organization, Town and Country Planning Organization, National Zoo Authority, Ministry of Tourism, Ministry of Skill Development and Entrepreneurship, Development Authorities, Smart City Corporations across the country, other Public Departments of the Government and many more to uncover.

While our predecessors did not suffer a crisis of natural resources in their time, it is inspiring to see the efforts they made to preserve them for upcoming generations. With the arrival of the Industrial Era, however, overexploitation of natural assets began, resulting in a complete collapse of traditional ethos for building a sustainable environment in which humans could live in peace with nature.

Yet, millennia-old architectural principles are still in use and will be for a long time to come because of their spiritual and cultural foundations. Contemporary Indian architecture's multi-ethnic nature makes it an intriguing field for future investigations and breakthroughs. Socio-cultural determinants are "Indianizing" contemporary and universalized architecture, assisting in the evolution of a modern Indian architectural character. India is destined to become Asia's epicenter of modern sustainable architecture.

In conclusion, the more I have studied and practiced sustainability, the more I have realized its parallel with the Vernacular Architecture, which establishes a relationship between people, climate and architecture. It demonstrates identity and sustainability. It reflects time, place and culture. The sustainable approach already exists in vernacular architecture. The constructions involved here are simple and can easily merge with nature. It is less costly as the materials are locally available, hence the transportation costs gets reduced. The important features of vernacular architecture are durability and versatility. The basic goal includes producing functional buildings. Vernacular traditions exist for different climates and cultures. It keeps our traditions alive. Vernacular architecture is shaped by a vast variety of elements from history and the rich vibrant culture, right form the times of the Ancient Alien Architects - **But that can be the agenda for another Book, may be next time!**